CONFIDENT SPEAKING

ALAN WOODHOUSE

A PRACTICAL GUIDE

Published in the UK and USA
in 2014 by Icon Books Ltd,
Omnibus Business Centre,
39–41 North Road,
London N7 9DP
email: info@iconbooks.com
www.iconbooks.com

Sold in the UK, Europe and Asia
by Faber & Faber Ltd,
Bloomsbury House,
74–77 Great Russell Street,
London WC1B 3DA
or their agents

Distributed in South Africa
by Jonathan Ball,
Office B4, The District,
41 Sir Lowry Road,
Woodstock 7925

Distributed in Australia and
New Zealand
by Allen & Unwin Pty Ltd,
PO Box 8500,
83 Alexander Street,
Crows Nest,
NSW 2065

Distributed in Canada
by Penguin Books Canada,
90 Eglinton Avenue East, Suite 700,
Toronto,
Ontario M4P 2Y3

Distributed to the trade in the USA
by Consortium Book Sales
and Distribution
The Keg House,
34 Thirteenth Avenue NE, Suite 101,
Minneapolis, MN 55413-1007

ISBN: 978-184831-679-9

Typeset in Avenir by Marie Doherty

Printed and bound in the UK by Clays Ltd, St Ives plc

About the author

Alan Woodhouse is a voice, acting, communication and public speaking coach. He trained at the Guildhall School of Music & Drama and Central School of Speech & Drama. He now runs a private consultancy in London, training everyone from actors to business executives to media professionals. His business clients come from major financial institutions, government departments and international corporations.

Alan's work in theatre has taken him to Paris, Rome, Berlin, Vienna, and Aix-en-Provence. He has also worked at the Royal Court Theatre, Shakespeare's Globe and the Young Vic in London.

Contents

Introduction   1

PART ONE: The basics   **5**
  1. Breathing   7
  2. Diction   13
  3. Rhythm   23
  4. Gravitas   27

PART TWO: Presentations – preparation and planning   **33**
  5. What is the message I want (or need) to deliver to my audience?   37
  6. How do I choose the best words to tell my story?   41
  7. Scripting the presentation   49
  8. Delivery   59
  9. Be prepared   73

PART THREE: Speeches for specific events   **85**
  10. The wedding speech   87
  11. Doing a reading   123

PART FOUR: Speeches for all occasions   **137**

12. The leaving speech   139
13. The interview   151
14. Meetings and conversations   165

Conclusion   179
Appendix: Speaker's Toolkit   187
Index   199

Notes   205
Other titles in the Practical Guides series   209

Introduction

Who are you and who am I?

You are an everyman, or woman. You are someone who thinks about their voice, and is aware that it doesn't always behave the way you would like it to. Maybe you hate hearing yourself on a voicemail message. Or maybe you've spoken in a meeting or at a wedding and felt that the passion in your voice didn't match the passion in your heart. Maybe you've asked for a pay rise, only to have your voice quaver and betray your lack of self-confidence. This book is for you.

We can all listen to someone else and think that in some way or other they make a better job of it than we would. They choose the right words, make the right sounds, smile the right smile. And this negative attitude can be vicious. Other people may take the wind out of our sails, but self-criticism is lethal to confident speaking.

This book is full of practical exercises and ideas that you can start to use straight away. Some techniques will need a little time and energy and patience to master, but it might surprise you how quickly you pick up some useful skills. Just five minutes of good preparation can transform tragedy into triumph. The key to confident speaking is rekindling a belief in yourself. Your voice is just as good as anyone else's. It just needs bringing out.

First, I'm going to introduce you to some breathing exercises, to help you relax and find your most confident voice. You'll then learn how to explore what you want to say and how to find the best way to say it. I'll advise you on how to write speeches and presentations, and even talk a little bit about how to deal with the dreaded PowerPoint. You may be considering a new work position or role, one where you will be in front of an audience more often, needing to project and display total confidence and ease. You may be just out of university and expecting a whole raft of interviews that need your full attention. Or you may already be in a position where you have to speak publicly, but just want to learn to do it better. Either way, you need to prepare yourself, and this book will help you make best use of every opportunity.

Some situations allow us to plan quite precisely the words we have to speak, so we can make notes and rehearse. Other situations are more open-ended and need us to react as the moment demands. Together, we will go through ideas and exercises to help you face all of these eventualities, and you will learn how to build structures that can underpin these most stress-inducing events. Finally, at the end of the book you'll find a Speaker's Toolkit. This contains a range of ideas and exercises – many of them only taking a minute or two – that you can pick and choose to use to build up your strength and give you more skills, and call on whenever you need them.

So who am I? I am a voice, acting, communication and public speaking coach. My job, essentially, is to get either myself or the people I coach to the right place at the right time, and in the right frame of mind. (And in some cases, in the right costume, and having learnt the script.) The venue can be anything from a theatre to a TV studio to a church to an office meeting room to your favourite bar.

My job is to advise, suggest, encourage, support and educate. And anything else you can think of that might help you get to your confident speaking moment in the best shape and spirits. The only thing I can't do is do it for you.

Right from the beginning, my best advice is to start to talk, out loud, about the plans you need to make. Speaking needs all of our energies: mental, emotional, and physical.

You could use your mobile phone to record your voice, a voice recorder on your computer, a digital recorder or even an old cassette-player. Use what is most portable and easiest to handle. Holding something in your hand, or at least having something there in front of you, will give you a focal point. You may feel less self-conscious than just talking into mid-air. You'll have a dual experience: you'll hear your voice in real-time, as you speak, and you'll get the recorded version. So I strongly recommend that when you're doing the exercises in this book you always record and listen back to them.

The recorded version of our voice can take a bit of time to adjust to, as it's not the version we are used to hearing. Our ears are on the outside of our body so we do hear the sounds we make. But, at the same time, we also experience sensations inside our throat and head and elsewhere in our body – breath is moving, our vocal cords vibrate, our lips and tongue shape the words we speak. So when we listen to a recorded version of our voice it can sound quite different to how we thought it sounded.

There are important points for us to notice here. Most of us are prone to being self-critical of our own voice, which is usually less than helpful and potentially destructive. When we are overwhelmed with strong emotions – especially negative ones, like self-criticism – our breathing muscles tend to tighten. If our breathing is tight and tense, then our voice will be tight and tense. To find our best, most confident voice, we need to find relaxation and deep breathing. There really is no such thing as a 'good' voice or a 'bad' voice. Just as we get fit by exercising other parts of our body you can get vocally fit if you do some of the training outlined in this book.

When you record your thoughts and ideas you can try out different ways of saying the same thing. As you listen back you'll like some options better than others. You could begin scripting your material by using the options you like. It can be hard to know if we've chosen the right words until we hear those words spoken. Just reading them in our head will not give us the same experience. Spoken language can be quite different to written language, and what looks quite perfect on the page may well sound less than ideal. As you use your voice, and choose what you want to say, you'll fight any fears you might have. You are about to begin your journey towards achieving your own best confident speaking. I think we should get started.

PART ONE
The basics

In this section we are going to work through the fundamentals of confident speaking: mastering your breath and articulation, teaching you how to get rhythmic energy in your speech and helping you relax. By the time we're done, you should feel confident that the words you speak will trip off your tongue easily and clearly.

1. Breathing

The first and most important tool to harness in terms of confident speaking is your breath. Just because you decide in your head that you want to say something, doesn't mean your body will fall into line. Bodies can be very stubborn! So we have to train them to do what we want.

Think what you would do if there was a food shortage: you'd go to the shops, grab as much food as possible, lock it away in your store cupboard and save it for the rainy day you hope will never come. Speaking is the same. When you want your voice to be on its best behaviour – that important meeting, presentation, wedding speech or interview – your body will want to store up some extra supplies of breath. Your body understands that you need a good supply of breath to speak with confidence.

We're all full of good intentions, aren't we? Your body is trying to do right by you, to help you prepare for that important moment. Let's go back to the food stocking-up scenario. Instinctively, you don't want to start using the precious food too soon, not until it's really necessary. In the same way, your body gets a bit too keen on hanging on to all that breath it has taken in. Why give it all away without a bit of a fight? And this is the problem. We need the breath to flow – it's the basic energy that gives life to your voice.

REMEMBER THIS!!! We have a tendency to hold our breath when we are thinking, when we are listening and when we are waiting, especially if we're busy and lots of things need our attention. When you feel the stress levels rising, remind yourself to multi-task. Tell yourself, 'I can breathe as I think, and as I listen, and as I wait.'

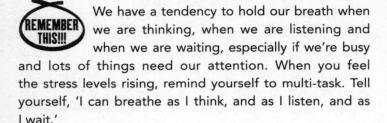

TRY IT NOW! First, gently but firmly tighten the muscles in your stomach, but not too strongly; you shouldn't feel ill. Now speak out loud the numbers one to ten. Remember what it feels like, and what it sounds like to speak with this tension in your stomach. Now release those poor old muscles. You should be able to feel that they can freely move again and speak the numbers again, with your stomach relaxed. It sounds different, doesn't it? And I hope it feels better too!

Breathing exercises

We're going to do some breathing exercises to get you relaxed, confident and with enough breath to project your voice. You need to make sure that two areas in particular can move freely – the stomach and the ribs.

STOMACH EXERCISE 1

Place one hand on your stomach – the centre of the palm around your belly button – so you can feel your stomach move as you breathe. Imagine there is a tiny bit of fluff on the hand that's resting on your stomach, and you want to gently blow it off. The sound you'll make is 'pppphhhhh'. Your lips will be softly together and you'll feel your stomach move a bit.

Next, focus on an object about an arms length away from you. There's a bit of fluff on it too. Gently but firmly, blow away the fluff: 'pppphhhhhh'. You'll feel your stomach move a bit more energetically. Because the distance is larger, you automatically generate more energy.

Why am I doing this?

You are waking up the breathing muscles in the stomach so that you can breathe more deeply. Picture your lungs as roughly pear-shaped, so the biggest bits are near the bottom. If we breathe using mostly the upper part of the chest – nearer to the smallest parts of the 'pear' – we only get a shallow and short-lived breath. This is not good for projecting a confident voice.

Our breathing muscles are no different to any other muscles, in that they get lazy and out of condition. If the breathing muscles in the stomach and the ribcage area are not able to move flexibly and energetically then our voices will tend to sound flat and uninteresting, which will not help us to be confident speakers.

In the second exercise you will explore how long you can sustain your outgoing breath. You'll find that the secret to breathing in well is to breathe out in a strong and forthright way. Putting it simply, the better you breathe out, the better you'll breathe in!

STOMACH EXERCISE 2

Place one hand on your stomach and silently count eight beats as you breathe out. Your stomach will get smaller and your hand will move inwards. As you breathe in your stomach will expand and your hand will move outwards. Never rush when you are breathing in, take as long as your body needs.

Try breathing out for ten beats, breathe in again, then out for twelve beats. Remember, you control the speed of the beats, but I'd recommend about two beats per second. The longer you can breathe <u>out</u>, without making yourself panic or feel ill, the more you will be aware of your stomach moving energetically as you breathe <u>in</u>. Try adding another two beats to your out-breath, but don't rush, take it gently. As you continue to practise this exercise you should be able to increase the number of beats that you can comfortably breathe out.

 Breathing more deeply will also help you to relax the upper chest and your vocal and articulation muscles. This means that they can move more freely and flexibly and your confident voice will not

10

get locked away in a tense throat. That's a major reason why the breathing exercises are so important.

RIBS EXERCISE 1

Your ribs should join with your stomach to free up a stronger and more sustained flow of breath energy. This breath will help you to make a confident and healthy sound.

Prop this book up on a table so you have both hands free, and lift both arms in the air, stretching them towards the ceiling. With your right hand, grab hold of your left wrist. Your right hand will begin to gently pull and stretch your left arm upwards, until you feel the left side of your ribcage and back begin to stretch out. Stay stretched as you silently breathe out to the count of eight, and stay stretched as you take time to breathe in. Don't rush.

Stay stretched as you breathe out again to the count of ten, and as you breathe in. Keep adding two beats to your out-breath. See if you can get to twenty, but don't worry if at first you can't. Your body will need time to get used to these new exercises.

When you've completed your stretches on your left side, repeat the exercise on your right side. Start by holding your right wrist with your left hand.

RIBS EXERCISE 2

Put your hands on your ribcage so that you can feel both sides moving. Breathe out to the count of eight: notice your ribcage getting smaller. Visualize the movements as being like an umbrella opening and closing. The umbrella opens up as you breathe in and closes as you breathe out.

Breathe out to the count of ten, then take time to breathe in. Continue doing this, adding two beats to your out-breath each time. See if you can get to twenty, but don't worry if you can't. With practice you will improve.

 Don't worry if you feel a *little* breathless after doing these exercises, as long as you don't feel ill, and as long as the breathless feeling doesn't last for more than a few moments. If you're struggling you can choose to build up your stamina bit by bit. Twelve beats today, fourteen tomorrow.

 Remember that it's virtually impossible to breathe really badly if you are lying flat-out: on the floor, on a bed, wherever feels comfortable. You are being supported literally from head to toe. You might as well relax and let the floor take the weight of your body. Let the floor do all the hard work. You'll breathe more freely if you do.

---

2. Diction

Tension is a bit like hot air: it tends to rise. Starting around the belly button, it can move into the chest and up into the throat itself. When that happens we can feel as if we are frozen in the moment and unable to move. Good breathing will help us to relax the tension that can cripple our confidence, but to achieve good diction we need to exercise our articulation muscles and learn how to control them.

We've all suffered from the nerves that can leave us not even able to speak our own name without tripping over the words, or trying to speak faster than our mouths can go, and ending up mumbling and being asked to repeat ourselves. You may recognize some comments from my clients:

I need to improve my diction; I need to stop being so lazy and open my mouth more when I speak.

I speak clearly but too fast because I want to get everything out at the same time.

I speak with a lot of passion: I get excited and the audience gets confused.

I actually don't feel that nervous, but I do tend to mumble.

You can skim-read but you can't 'skim-speak'. The physical act of speaking takes time and energy; it takes place in real time not 'thinking' time. We think much faster than we can speak. When we rush in our heads our bodies tend to move more slowly. Our muscles tense up. We want to go faster and end up going slower.

The heat of the moment can cause us to lose control – or fear that we are losing control – and the pacing of our speech becomes erratic. Telling ourselves to 'slow down' has little effect. It's not that we're not listening, just that somehow the instruction doesn't reach the control centre.

Going to the gym

To speak clearly we need to look at some articulation exercises, which I usually refer to as 'taking your mouth to the gym'. We know the rest of our body needs exercise, and for clarity and control of diction we need to exercise our mouths.

Words have a mixture of vowel and consonant sounds, but it is usually the articulation of the consonants that gives us the precise meaning.

ARTICULATION EXERCISE 1

Say 'one two three four five'. Do it smoothly, as if the five numbers were part of the same phrase. Say it again, but looking in a mirror. Be honest: what do you see? Here's what you should be looking out for:

Do your lips come together at all? They should do, when you say the first sound of the first word, the 'www' of 'one'. (I'm writing some of these consonants with three letters rather than just one because I wwwant to encourage you to rrreally give them time to sssound, and not to rush them.)

Can you see the tip of your tongue pointing up towards the roof of your mouth as you make the 'nnn' at the end of the first word? You might see it touching the back of your upper teeth. The tip of your tongue should also touch the back of your upper teeth at the beginning of the next word – the 'tuh' of 'two'. If you can do this you'll get a good, clear sound.

Do your upper teeth touch the upper side of your tongue? They should as you say the 'th' of 'three'.

Does the tip of the tongue bend backwards for the 'rrr' in 'three'?

Do your upper teeth touch your lower lip? This should happen three times, when you say the 'fff's and 'vvv's in 'four' and 'five'.

What a lot of action for just five little words. That's a lot of movement for the tongue and the lips, as well as the teeth. Each movement takes time and energy, and everyone will have their own variations as to just how each move is made. But if you don't see much movement at all when you look in your mirror, then odds are your articulation will not be as clear as you would like it to be. You need to practise, so let's move on to the second exercise.

ARTICULATION EXERCISE 2
Mouth 'one two three four five' silently. Move your tongue and your lips but do it as silently as possible. Not even whispering. You will hear a little clicking sounds when you make any plosive sound, like the 'tuh' at the beginning of 'two'. Take time to shape the consonants.

This little exercise can work wonders on your pronunciation. By articulating silently we can focus on the movements of the tongue and lips that will give us good clarity. And it reminds us just how long it takes for our mouth to move from one sound to another.

No one really needs to know you're doing this exercise. You could even try it sitting on the bus – silently shaping the words of the newspaper or book you're reading – or listening to someone on the car radio and silently articulating what they say. Think about what you will say at the beginning of your meeting or interview and silently articulate your first words. Try using different words to say the same thing. Which do you like best? One version might roll off the tongue more easily.

When convenient, end this second articulation exercise by moving from silence to speaking out loud. First, shape the words silently, and then immediately speak the same words out loud. Practise for five minutes every day and you will soon hear some new clarity in your speech.

ARTICULATION EXERCISE 3

Silently mouth the words one to five reeeeeally slooooooowly, and then the words six to ten really quickly. Alternate mouthing five slowly and five quickly all the way up to 30.

In the first two articulation exercises you are tuning-up your articulation muscles, like tuning an instrument. Here you are beginning to control the pacing – a key factor in being an engaging speaker.

 Take care – it is all too easy to start off with a clear difference between the slow and the quick and then to settle into a medium pace.

You can use this next exercise on the actual words and ideas you need to deliver, whether that's a pre-written speech, a poem or a presentation. Clients often find it useful to break down the text into manageable phrases. The three things you'll want to focus on are:

1. Getting the words into your mouth and into your body. They are not just an intellectual idea; you are physically committing yourself to them.

2. Remembering that this is a real time experience of speaking: it will take you longer to speak with clarity and confidence than it would if you were reading the words in your head.

3. Remembering that you control the speed at which you speak.

ARTICULATION EXERCISE 4

For this exercise you will speak out loud: the first phrase will be slow and the second will be quick, the third phrase slow, and the fourth quick, and so on. You might decide you'd like to speak at different speeds when you are actually doing the speech. That's not a problem at all. The purpose of this exercise is to practise controlling your speed. Having mastered that you can speak in whatever way suits the occasion.

You could use the text below (Prime Minister William Gladstone's 1853 budget speech) as a practice text, or work straight away with your own ideas.

SLOW	QUICK
I scarcely dare to look at the clock	reminding me, as it must
how long, how shamelessly	I have trespassed on the time of the Committee.
All I can say in apology is closely to the topics	that I have endeavoured to keep which I had before me.
These are the proposals of the government.	They may be approved, or they may be condemned.

As soon as you have spoken your slow-quick version, speak the whole text again. This time concentrate on what you want to *say*, rather than the pace. Expect to hear a variety of speed and to feel in control of your message.

As always with these exercises, you must be prepared to practise.

Is my accent holding me back?

The quotes below come from people who have contacted me wanting advice and help:

> *My CV is judged as good, but my spoken English is not making an impact in interviews.*

> *Improving my accent would improve my business performance.*

> *My career progression is restricted because of my voice and accent.*

> *English is not my first language and even after having studied and lived in the UK for years, I still feel my accent is much too 'foreign'.*

Wherever we're from, we have an accent. It's an unfortunate fact of life that occasionally this can lead to people judging us, one way or another. It would be a very boring world if we all spoke in the same way, but while I certainly don't think the aim should be to eradicate your accent there are two things I would encourage you to give some thought to. First and foremost it will be difficult for you to achieve confident speaking without good clarity. And secondly, I want you to feel that you are making the best of your voice; that you can control it, and that it does what you want it to. If you were a pianist or violinist you would want to play more than one tune, however beautiful that tune might be. Your voice is an instrument capable of great variety, and it would be a shame not to extend your repertoire.

Good diction demands that we have strong and clear consonants, but the vowel sounds also need some exercising. We may shape some vowels with our lips but for English vowels the shape that the tongue makes is usually most important. Vowels are the spaces between the consonants. If the consonants sound too close together you will not get good clarity.

First, clench your jaw, and with your mouth tightly closed count to ten. Do you hear how constricted the vowels sound? That's because the space in your mouth and throat is restricted.

Now let your mouth drop open, and for a few seconds gently place your thumb in the space between your upper and lower teeth. Move your thumb away from your teeth, but keep the space between the teeth open, and again count to ten. Do you hear how much clearer the vowels are? You've given them some space to relax and open out into.

VOWEL EXERCISES

1. For each English vowel your tongue will make a different shape in your mouth. Look in the mirror and say the word 'car'. Now say the word 'key'. Can you see that your tongue needs to make a different shape for each vowel – the 'ah' of 'car' and the 'ee' of 'key'?

2. Some words can be pronounced with two vowels, one after the other in quick succession. Here's an example: take the vowel you hear when you say the word 'head' and quickly follow it with the vowel from the word 'hit' and you'll have your two vowels for the word 'hey'.

Practise with these words to encourage good, clear articulation. Listen for two different vowels in each word of each sequence:

'hi, how, here'
'way, why, where'
'lay, lie, low'
'may, my, mow'
'now, no, near'

These exercises are not about 'correct' pronunciation, as there is no such thing. They are about encouraging your tongue to move smoothly and flexibly as you change from one vowel to another. If your tongue does not move freely you will find it difficult to speak with clarity.

REMEMBER THIS!!!

A good accent will always offer us the freedom to have rhythmic vitality in our speech.

3. Rhythm

We can think of rhythm as a kind of pulse or heartbeat: it is the lifeblood of our message. It could be a very steady beat until the temperature starts to rise, and the stronger emotion increases the pulse. There are two things that we should focus on. First, if the rhythm is too regular for too long a time we might not get our message across effectively. That could mean that the water is always calm and our audience are lulled to sleep, or that everything is stormy and choppy and we seem to reach a new climax in our story every five seconds. Secondly, we need the rhythmic energy of our speech to match the rhythmic energy of the material we are delivering. If our voice sounds dull then people might think that what we're saying is dull. We want to be able to access a wide range of emotion when we speak.

Any word with more than one syllable will have a natural rhythm, which consists of stressed and unstressed syllables (or heavier and lighter ones, if you prefer to think of them that way). The word 'rhythm' has two syllables. When we speak the word, the stress, or weight, is usually on the 'rhy', the first syllable. The second syllable is the light one. But 'inspire' also has two syllables, and 'spire' is usually the heavy syllable, the stressed one. The first syllable is light.

Most of this you may not need to think about. But often when we are more tense or anxious, or if we feel a bit unsure about what we are going to say or how we might say it, the rhythm of our speech gets flattened out. So to prepare ourselves for confident speaking it's good to retune our awareness of rhythm.

Take your own name. 'My name is Alan, what's yours?' If I wanted to hum the rhythm of these words I'd get, 'MM mm mm MM mm mm MM?', where the letters in capitals represent the heavier syllables of the phrase. ('MY name is ALan what's YOURS?') For my name, I'd stress the first syllable, the 'AL' part. But if, for example, my name were 'Marcel' I would stress the second half – the 'CEL' part – and keep the 'Mar' quite light.

I'll take another simple phrase: 'Yesterday was Friday.' 'MM mm mm mm MM mm.' You could use the same technique on a phrase from a newspaper or a book, or some notes for a presentation or speech you are working on.

You want to hear the contrast between 'light' and 'heavy' syllables. If you're feeling really daring, sing your phrase. You'll hear even more clearly the rhythmic energy of your words. Music can be very useful in encouraging us to find new tunes and new colours for our voices.

Take three short phrases from a text – a newspaper or the back of the cereal packet, it doesn't matter – and hum the rhythm of the words. Then, return to the beginning and speak the text. I hope you hear the liveliness of the rhythm as you speak.

RHYTHM EXERCISE 1

I call this exercise 'The Stressing Game'. Pick up a newspaper, a book, or some work material, and take three phrases of the text. Ask yourself which word might be the most important.

Is it 'The CAT sat on the mat'? Or 'The cat SAT on the mat'? Or 'The cat sat ON the mat'? Each time we decide on a different word to stress, we change the meaning. It might be just a small change, or it might be more major. Is it that the *cat* sits on the mat, rather than the dog? Is it that the cat is *sitting*, rather than lying? Or is it that the cat is sitting *on* the mat, rather than under the mat?

Work with your text and try different versions. Which is the most powerful way to tell the story?

4. Gravitas

I'd like some more depth in my voice.

My voice is too high.

There are two distinct ways that we might experience 'height' or 'depth' of voice. It could relate to the musical pitch we are using. Think of the tune of 'Happy Birthday'. 'Birth' is a higher pitch than 'day'. 'To' is even higher. We might be using quite a high pitch as we speak, which could leave us open to comments that we 'sound young' or are not delivering our message with due weight, or even that we sound too emotional.

But, and this is more likely, height of voice also relates to what we usually refer to as resonance. If we are breathing deeply and getting some good relaxation in our chest and neck and throat we will be able to find some of that richness and depth of voice that is often labelled as 'gravitas'. And rather than trying to push your voice down to an uncomfortable pitch, finding some chest resonance, as it is termed, is a much better option. Chest resonance will help you find your gravitas.

Three relaxation exercises for gravitas
Try out each of these and you'll find the one that suits you best.

1. Lie flat on the floor. Bend your legs so that your feet are flat on the floor and your knees point up towards the ceiling. Put a book underneath your head to help keep your neck relaxed. Accept that you are fully supported, head to toe. Place one hand on your stomach and feel your hand move downwards as you breathe out. Feel it lift up as the new breath comes in to fill you. Say 'ffffff' as you breathe out. Sing 'mmmmmm' on the next out-breath. Place your other hand on the upper chest. Sing 'mmmmmm' again and feel the warmth and vibration of the energy in your upper chest. Make a gentle but quite fast, rocking movement with the hand touching the chest as you 'mmmmmm' again. If your voice sounds richer and more powerful you'll know you've found the right movement.

2. Sit on a dining chair and then let your whole upper body flop over so you're looking at the floor. Your arms will hang down and your hands will dangle on the floor. You will feel your stomach moving against the top of your legs as you breathe. Your head will feel very heavy and your throat will feel relaxed, as if you're about to yawn. Say 'ffffff' as you breathe out. Then sing 'mmmmmm' on the next out-breath. Repeat 'mmmmmm' on three more out-breaths. Come back, very smoothly, to sitting upright, allowing your spine to straighten up vertebra by vertebra, from the bottom to the top.

When you're sitting back up, sing 'mmmmmm' on the next out-breath. Place one hand on the upper chest so that you can be aware of your voice vibrating. Repeat the 'mmmmmm' three more times.

3. Sit on a dining chair, lift up your arms and do the stretches in the first rib exercise detailed earlier in this section. Then place your hands on your ribs and sing 'mmmmmm'. Feel your ribs move inwards as you sing. Repeat three times. Now place one hand on your stomach to check that you're still moving freely there, and one hand on your upper chest to feel the good strong energy as you sing 'mmmmmm' again.

Why are you doing this?

To get a bit of 'chest' or 'bass' resonance in your voice, which is the deep resonant sound that most people hanker after and love listening to. We want people to listen to us when we speak. We want them to have some expectation that we could say something worth listening to, and worth giving attention to. We are judgemental about the sounds that attract us or repel us. Speaking with a depth of sound usually signals to the listener that it is worth staying in touch.

Is your voice unhappy?

Here are some common complaints I hear from my clients:

Sometimes towards the end of the day my voice feels tired.

I am a public speaker, but tend to lose my voice half an hour into a presentation.

I'm sometimes asked if I have a sore throat when talking on the telephone.

My voice seems to come from the back of the throat.

I lose my voice quite often. It sometimes hurts to speak by the afternoon.

I find that I'm straining my voice so that I can be heard, which is making my voice sound harsher than normal.

If I attempt to speak louder my throat becomes dry and sore very quickly.

We all have our vocal habits. Some of those habits might be literally giving us vocal distress. Your voice should not hurt as you speak, or afterwards. If you've been shouting at a football match and suffer afterwards at least you'll know why. If you continue the shouting on a regular basis, you could end up with a more serious problem. But if you are talking quite 'normally' and have concerns you need to find some answers.

REMEMBER THIS!!!

Here are some simple ways to help a voice that is suffering:

1. Make sure that you are getting some good vocal exercise by working with the ideas in this chapter. And refer to the Speaker's Toolkit at the back of this book.

2. If you do nothing else, regularly spend ten to fifteen minutes relaxing flat-out on the floor. Check that you are breathing well, and sustain some 'ffffff' and 'mmmmmm' sounds as you breathe out.

3. When you are in your car, play the radio or some music and sing. You don't even need to know the words, humming the tunes will do just fine. Don't try and sing too loud. Give yourself plenty of time to breathe. And stop immediately if your voice feels tired or sore.

4. Singing in the shower or the kitchen is also recommended – anywhere that you can feel relaxed and have the chance to warm up your vocal muscles.

5. Whispering can be one of the most tiring ways to use our voice. If you have a cold or your energy is low, it's a great temptation to grumble down in the lowest part of our voice. Resist this temptation and instead pitch your voice a little higher than usual. You'll find it easier to sustain your speaking through a busy day.

6. Remember that coffee, tea, and alcohol can have a dehydrating effect on our body. Any extra caffeine can make our stressed nerves feel even more hyper, and encourage a faster breathing pattern. A glass of water will often be your best option.

7. Just as it's a good idea to warm up the body at the beginning of the day, so it makes sense to warm down at the end of the day. Some humming along to a favourite song would do the trick.

8. And finally, if any discomfort persists, you need to get a medical opinion. There could be a very simple explanation. The production of voice is dependant on a fair number of moving parts. Sometimes a drop of medicine is needed to 'oil the wheels', so to speak.

IF YOU REMEMBER ONE THING If you play a sport, think back to the first time you kicked the ball, swam a length of the pool or ran a race. Were you brilliant on that very first day? Didn't you need time to develop? Developing confident vocal skills is just the same. You need goals, you need a plan, and you need patience.

PART TWO
Presentations – preparation and planning

At the beginning of this book I wanted to encourage you to learn to prepare yourself physically for your confident speaking moment. We've been looking at breathing more deeply to keep you relaxed and give you a strong and confident sound. And you have some exercises under your belt to help you consider your diction and clarity, and to encourage you to speak with good rhythmic energy so that your voice will engage an audience. I also wanted you to be able to look after your voice, if it feels tired or in need of a 'pick-me-up'. There are more exercises on these topics in the Speaker's Toolkit at the end of the book, should you feel the need to further extend those skills.

We now need to consider in some detail some of the different speaking situations you may find yourself in, starting with giving a presentation. I want to guide you, step by step, through to the 'event' itself. Using a voice recorder will be important and useful, but there is obviously a good deal more intellectual work that may be necessary. Here are some concerns clients have told me they need help with:

I become very nervous when giving presentations,
especially speaking to a large group; I forget everything
I have planned.

I feel very self-conscious when speaking formally.

I got so anxious I walked out of the room before I could
start my presentation.

I am confident generally but when I have to stand up in
public to speak I completely lose my voice.

I find that my brain works faster than my voice, and
I become rather breathless with nerves just prior
to delivery.

We are all pretty good at imagining the future, aren't we? But does it usually turn out like we imagine? Probably not, otherwise we could all be millionaires. So we should do everything we can to be prepared for all eventualities, even if it takes time to do.

I think it can be productive to think of anything we have to say, whether it's a presentation or a speech, or just a conversation as 'telling a story'. It could be a story about government policy or a newlywed couple, or it could be a story about Goldilocks and the three bears, as you'll see.

Deciding on the content of your story, and deciding how you want or need to *tell* your story are two very different things. I would advise you to keep reminding yourself of that point, otherwise you could quite unnecessarily burden yourself with a bad script. If you were an actor, for example, your script would often be fixed, but you would still have many options regarding how you performed the material.

So let's decide that we have three relatively separate questions to think about when creating the script in the first place:

1. What is the message I want or need to deliver to my audience? I need to generate material.

2. How do I choose the best words to tell my story and do I need to incorporate other audio or video material? I need to script my material.

3. How might I speak/perform/deliver/act, in order to tell my story in as full and confident way as possible? I need to rehearse so that I am ready for my performance.

5. What is the message I want (or need) to deliver to my audience?

Right from the beginning the best advice is to start to talk, out loud, about the plans you need to make. And I believe you'll find it most useful if you record your voice. You'll have the chance to get used to the sounds you make, both in the act of speaking and when listening back to your recording. If something about your voice really bothers you – it doesn't feel powerful enough, varied enough, clear enough – you can start to deal with it. But anchor yourself in the fact that all you are doing at first is surveying the situation, not thinking about the kind of performance you are going to give. And if you can begin to listen to yourself in a more objective way, you'll find it very useful. You could play different 'roles'. You could be the audience member who knows nothing and needs you to take nothing for granted, or you could be the audience member who knows quite a lot and would prefer you to cut to the chase.

RECORDING EXERCISE 1

Get your voice recorder and begin to talk. Ask yourself some very specific questions about your presentation. All the usual 'w's are there. What are you talking about? Why are you talking about it? Why is it you (rather than someone else) who is doing the talking? Who are you talking to? Where are you speaking? When are you doing the talk? How long do you have for your talk? Is all the material spoken or will there be visual or audio material? Who decides what will actually be said?

There are two main reasons for doing this exercise. First, you will have made a start, not just by thinking (and perhaps worrying), but by being active and doing something practical. You are starting to anchor yourself in some facts, telling yourself what you know about the plans for the event. And secondly, once you are clear about what needs to be done, you can begin to make decisions about how you're going to do it.

Turn the recorder off. That's quite enough for your first recording. If at all possible, and this will depend on individual circumstances, don't listen to your recording for 24 hours. Why? Because it will give you a bit of distance, and allow you to be a kinder, more objective listener.

RECORDING EXERCISE 2
This exercise could be done after you have listened to your first recording, but doesn't have to be.

Talk about your feelings about doing the speech. It's a stream of consciousness, so think about the situation from every possible angle. What is your biggest fear? Speak it out loud. What is the worst thing that could happen? Go to town on this one. Get it all out in the open. Would the world really come to an end if you stumble over one word? Have you done one of these events before and not enjoyed it?

Or been terrified and forgotten everything you'd planned? Is this something that you've been hoping for and dreaming about for a long time? Could the dream quickly turn into a nightmare if you don't make some decisions about the event soon? Be honest with yourself about any less-than-perfect past experiences, and then move forward and firmly focus yourself on planning for the future.

RECORDER EXERCISE 3

For this exercise I want you to focus on being totally practical. Give yourself some more details about the event. Consider your audience: what do they know? Are they all equally knowledgeable? Do you think they will want to hear what you want to tell them? If your audience has a strong reason for hearing your story, you will have an easier job. If someone is calling out, 'fire!' I don't think we would be judging them on their quality of voice, their choice of words or their pacing. We might think they could shout louder, or could have started shouting earlier. But as long as you manage to get out of the building alive, you'll probably be eternally grateful to them. What people expect from us is totally dependent on the situation, so take some time to talk through yours.

When you listen back to your recordings are you hearing someone who is clear about the story that needs telling? That's all you need to know to pass happily onto the next stage.

6. How do I choose the best words to tell my story?

Let's take a very familiar story as our example. 'Once upon a time, there were three bears ...'

There are lots of versions of this, as with most fairy stories. We could tell the story quite simply. There were the three bears. They make porridge but it's too hot to eat. So they go out. They forget to lock the door. Goldilocks enters the house. Eats porridge. Breaks a chair. Goes to sleep on a bed. The bears come back. They are not happy. Goldilocks makes a hasty retreat.

If I told the story using those words it's perhaps not very interesting. It's lacking in detail and I'm not convinced I would easily captivate an audience. But I would like to encourage you to think about the value of simplicity. It seems counter-intuitive, but we can feel more engaged and more interested if the author has not done all the work for us, because we can use our imagination to fill in the gaps.

Haven't we all sat on a bus or train listening in to someone's conversation? We don't mean to, of course, but if they will be so loud it can't be helped. We don't know these people. If they sit behind us, we won't know what they look like. We hear a voice. We hear some words. We conjure up our own picture. And probably our story is far more colourful than the 'real' one. We'll never know, so it's not a problem.

I once heard a lady on a bus say: 'I can't wait to get home and see what I'm wearing.' I've never worked that one out.

 So, we've looked at the 'bare bones' of the story of the three bears. What are the bare bones of your story? If you had no more than 30 seconds to give us an overview of what your (perhaps twenty-minute) story is, what would you say? Speak into your recorder.

Back to the bears. Now it seems to me that baby bear comes out of this worst of all. It wasn't his fault that his dippy parents forgot to lock the door. And letting a young child go out without his breakfast? Could they not have got up earlier, got the porridge on, and made sure it was cool enough for baby bear to eat, before making him go out in the cold? I'm elaborating a bit now; I don't think we know what the weather is like.

And so his porridge gets eaten, and his chair gets broken and his bed gets taken over. And just when he could do with a bit of a sleep, to get over all of this trauma, he has to start cleaning up all the mess Goldilocks has made (at least according to one of the versions I've been reading). Do they give him a piece of toast before he has to start scrubbing? I rest my case. Frankly I think the authorities should be called in to find that house-breaking, mess-making girl, Goldilocks. She could have at least wiped her feet.

As you can see, stories can be completely changed by the emphasis you put on them. I don't think we know much about the family background of Goldilocks. She might be trying to escape a violent step-parent, and the bears' house looks so warm and inviting, and she is so hungry and tired. And she's really sorry that she forgot to wipe her feet. So is she the hero or the villain? It's all in the telling.

 What is your story about? Does it have a definite beginning, middle and end? If so, do you have to begin at the beginning? Might it be more interesting to start at the end and work backwards?

 Speak into your recorder. Tell yourself in no more than one minute both how you might begin your story, and how you might end it. Now try to come up with a headline for your story. My headline for the Three Bears could be: '"I'LL NEVER LOOK AT A GIRL WITH BLONDE HAIR AGAIN!" CRIES HEARTBROKEN BABY BEAR'.

You might say, well that's all very well if your 'story' is full of emotion, but mine is full of facts – no one is going to want to listen to that. But I think we get fascinated with other people's fascination. We can feel passion because they feel passionate. I'll confess that, for instance, I am no sports fan, and am terminally ignorant about most sports. But I could be engaged with someone else's deep interest in the subject, as long as they didn't fill the story with jargon and terms that I didn't understand. And if they think it was the best night of their life when someone scored three goals in five minutes, and tell me their story with passion, I will share their joy and wave the flag.

Understanding your audience

So if you want me to listen to you, you have to understand some of my 'terms' as well as your own. How interested am I? How long have I got to listen? Is there a particular part of the story that might fascinate me most? Is there a 'hook' that can draw me in to your story?

Whatever you decide you need to say, you need to invest in the story with your imagination. If you feel you've made the ultimate decision, that these are the words to be spoken, remind yourself why you chose the words you did. You are speaking for a reason. Somebody needs to know what you already know. Or they need reminding. Or they need telling twice because they didn't take enough notice in the first place.

Do I need PowerPoint?

I still find clients battling with the same old PowerPoint problems. Too many screens, too many words and too many pictures on each screen. Too much temptation to use the screen as a memory-aid and just read the words out.

Rather than relying on it, think instead about how the screen can function for you. Pictures can tell parts of a story more effectively than words. If you need the audience to know what St. Paul's Cathedral looks like, it could be quicker to show them a picture. But why do you want them to know what St Paul's Cathedral looks like? Are you comparing it with Westminster Abbey? Then you might need two pictures.

People very easily look at the wrong thing – or, at least, they don't see what you want them to see. Give your audience too many things to look at, or think about, and you make life more difficult for yourself. If you want to point out that St. Paul's is a squatter shape and Westminster Abbey is longer – which is probably not remotely true – then it might be simpler to tell the audience.

You want the audience to focus on you, so that you have some control over the event. If there are too many distractions, you'll find that difficult. Some clients would rather like the attention to be drawn away from them and onto a screen. Sorry, but it won't work. If you are going to do the job well you have to make it clear that the space is yours. Otherwise nobody will listen to anything you say. And that will not help you find confidence as a public speaker.

Once your point is made, lose the picture if possible, unless you need to refer to it again. I know this sounds very pedantic, but keep bringing yourself back to the point: you are the centre of attention; everything else – a screen, music, a lighting effect – is to enhance what you do. You don't want the scenery to take over.

What do I do if there are lots of words on the screen?

If possible you show the text for as little time as possible. You yourself need to be very clear about exactly what the screen, with all of its words, is aiming to say. Find the nub of the message in each point. Sum up in as few words as possible. Stand or sit in the centre of the action, where you can see and be seen by everyone. Speak firmly and with great authority to signal that you are the boss, and that you come first. If you've been sitting, you could stand up for a few moments. Cover everything that you want the audience to know, and then lose that screen as soon as you can, preferably leaving a blank until you need to show them another slide.

What do I do if there are lots of pictures on the screen?

Plan to take the audience through the images in a very simple way. Working with clients on PowerPoint presentations, I always say: 'I am the man in the street. I know nothing about your industry – banking, gas and oil, whatever it might be – therefore I might not understand something that your audience understands very well.' But quite often when I say, 'Sorry I'm probably being very naïve, but what's that pink blob in the top-left corner?' the client decides that probably no one will understand what the pink blob is. You might have a mixed audience. Some get the pink blob, some don't. It's better to be on the safe side. Just as when there is a lot of text, tell the audience exactly what it is they are supposed to be looking at and seeing, and why they need to see whatever it is. Tell them which is image one and which is image two, and something of the logic of the order of the images.

7. Scripting the presentation

You decided what your story is in chapter five, and in chapter six we've been thinking about different ways to tell the story. Now you need to structure some notes so you can move into Part Four and start to rehearse.

Listen back to your recording, ask yourself the following questions and write or type out your answers:

1. Are there some phrases that you like? Write them down. Do you hear the story coming over in a clear and concise way? Write down what you feel is the best version.

2. Is it clear when you finish one point and start a new point? You don't want to squash all your content into one big point or it will be difficult for your audience to follow.

3. Do you need pictures or diagrams to help your audience understand your story? Make concise notes about what is necessary.

Stop listening to the material you've already recorded and start to record your voice again. Begin to speak out loud the notes you have just written. If you do need visual aids, include a description of exactly what you want people to see. Imagine that the audience are there in front of you; you need them to be very clear about what to look at.

Now focus on the shape of your talk. It will depend on the subject and the occasion as to what feels appropriate. And it will depend on you: what is your preferred way to tell your story? What is the style in which you feel most relaxed and confident?

Draw the shape of your talk:

- Do you start with a lot of ideas, and narrow them down in importance? If so, you have an upside-down triangle shape.

- Do you start with one idea and keep adding to and developing it? If so, the triangle is the right way up.

- Is there a very well-defined beginning and end, but the centre feels as if you curve or zigzag from point-to-point?

- Is it a series of straight lines that lead to the grand 'finale'?

It's a good idea to experiment – both on paper and vocally – with a variety of different ways of telling the same story or giving the same information. How does the story feel different if you change the order in which you make your points?

THINK ABOUT IT

Here are some questions that is useful to ask yourself at this stage:

• If you were listening to your presentation what might you need to know to expand the story, make it fuller and more complete?

• What might you not understand and need more information about?

• What could you work out for yourself without being given too much detail?

Structure

Here are some of the key points I recommend you think about when you're looking at structure:

• How many points should you make? Odd numbers are thought to be more memorable than even.

• What is the overall objective of your talk? What do you want the audience to understand above all?

• If you only had 30 seconds to do your speech or presentation, what would you choose to say?

We're now going to look at one of the simplest ways to structure a speech. Apparently Winston Churchill wrote out some of his speeches   somewhat like this   in phrases   rather than   complete sentences.

There are two main reasons why this is useful. We tend to speak in phrases rather than in full sentences, especially if we want to sound quite conversational. And if the writing is divided up into sections it's easier to see the shape of your message, where one sections ends and a new one starts. It will remind you to take time to pause so your audience will have a moment to digest what you've just told them and you'll have time for a breather. Some clients find it useful to put a different background colour behind each section of text, to make it even easier to see the shape of the speech when there's only a moment to glance down at the script.

You can try dividing your speech into a chart, as below.

good morning welcome thank you very much for coming
today we'll be talking about the price of fish small fish   big fish the most popular fish for the average customer and those 'special occasion' buys for high days and holidays
Christmas and Easter are very popular holiday times We like to entertain our family and friends We like to cook some special meals

Clients who fear they might too easily start off by talking about yesterday and end up talking about tomorrow, and not even notice they've gone off-topic will find this next layout useful. I call it 'The Motorway'. Think of the middle column as the motorway, and the right and left columns as the side roads. We might look to right or left and see an attractive sight. We've got plenty of time (we think), so let's go on a little wander. Have a little chat. Half an hour later and we're lost. 'Motorway? What motorway?' unfriendly natives say when we ask for directions. So if in your notes you can see quite clearly where the motorway is, and where it leads, it will help you to get back on track.

 Giovanni owns a bakery. He comes from a long line of bakers in Italy. He has been asked to talk about his business and the family history. But there are a lot of details he could potentially mention …

Giovanni is very proud of his family home in Italy, and his family has connections with the English town where he is doing his presentation, so he wants to be able to mention that in his speech. But he also wants to talk about the bread they bake, where the bread can be bought and why he believes it is so special. Then he'll invite the audience to have a taste of the samples he has brought with him. But he only has fifteen minutes, so unless he takes care not to wander off the motorway too many times

– especially at the beginning when he is talking about his family – he will be hard-pressed to finish in time, or he may have to miss out points that he believes his audience will find most interesting. So this is how he starts to structure his talk:

Side road	THE MOTORWAY	Side road
	Good evening It is a great pleasure to be here	
My grandfather lived in South Street In a pretty little house		In fact my grandfather lived in this town when he first came to England
I don't think the house is there now it was pulled down …	My family come from Naples That is where our family still has a bakery	
		Naples is famous for the volcano Vesuvius
Though in fact the people who supply the flour for us are not able to always send us the amount we need	So the recipe for our bread Has been passed down through the generations	Some of you maybe have been to Italy and seen Vesuvius
We have a second company …	We still use the same flour	

If Giovanni gets side-tracked and talks about all of the points from the 'side road' columns he won't finish his journey in time. He must make some tough choices and decide what the most important points he wants to make are. He may allow himself a few tiny detours but he must not stay away too long from the motorway.

Are you a little too fond of wandering away from your main points? Take a few moments to plot the motorway of your presentation.

Using cue cards is one simple way to remind yourself of the content, structure, and shape of your speech. You could have each separate section of the speech on a separate card, and rather than writing out all the words you're going to speak just have some brief notes to give you your cue.

When writing cue card verbs, or doing words, are very important: 'I inform', 'I educate', 'I simplify', 'I explain', 'I clarify', etc. What do you intend to do at each particular moment of your talk?

 If you have a clear idea of what you want to do, you have the best chance of finding a good way to do it.

We've looked at a one-column layout for your script, and a three-column version. But you might find that this next, two-column layout supports you best. The left-hand column tells you what you are doing – greeting the audience, welcoming them, etc. The right-hand column reminds you of the words you've chosen for your greeting or welcome. Rehearse with this layout. You might find that you only really need to refer to just one of the columns to feel well-supported. And that is what your layout must do – give you support and help to ease any anxieties. I would always advise that you include in your script any names you need to remember and other facts and figures.

I greet I welcome I introduce I give my job title I name the occasion	Good morning Great to see everyone I'm A.J. General Manager 'YOUR DISCUSSION DAY'
I inform I enthuse	Today's focus sharing You hear from us We hear from you
I outline programme	I'll start annual review as head of whole network Area managers give their news/views Southern branch BILL SMITH Western region BETTY REED Special challenges for new year priorities going forward
	Coffee break

REMEMBER THIS!!! Even if you don't want to use notes in your final presentation, the process of writing them helps to clarify your thoughts and find a shape for what you have to say. There is no perfect way to say anything – communication is trial and error.

8. Delivery

So far your brain and your fingers have been very busy, and now in this chapter we need to do some more exercises to ensure that you are fully prepared to speak in the most engaging way.

 Turn on your voice recorder.

You're a passionate person, aren't you? You feel things deeply? This recording is for your ears only. Record your comments on anything you really care about in life. Treat it like an audio diary, or a confessional. Give yourself two minutes to truly speak from your heart.

Now listen back to it. Isn't that the kind of vocal energy you want to hear when you're doing a presentation? It can be a quiet passion, slow and sustained. It can be a quick burst. Voicing your feelings can help you to increase your vocal repertoire. More variety, more colour, more tunes.

Passion would naturally sound in your voice if you were talking about your loved ones, your favourite music, the hobby that excites you. We want people to hear your passion even if you're delivering the driest list of facts. If you hear your voice full of energy, especially when you feel under pressure, you'll immediately increase your confidence. The passion in your voice will inspire you.

Here are some concerns clients have about their delivery:

> *When trying to make a point, I often find that my tone doesn't deliver the right sentiment.*

> *I want a voice people will want to listen to.*

> *I want to be impactful.*

> *I would like to turn heads when I start talking. People often don't realize that I actually said something.*

I'm going to suggest you do more of these little 'passion blogs', and I want you to think of each recording as a rehearsal.

KEY TERM

The word 'rehearsal' is interesting. The French word is *repetition* – which to English eyes tells its own story. The Italian word is *prova*, which means to try or test something.

Other languages doubtless have other takes on the word. I like the German word *probe*, which again means to test, but also, to English eyes, gives us an image of investigating something. It's interesting to have alternative points-of-view on the words we're using. We can 're-hear' what we have to say by 'repeating' it. We can 'try' different ways of saying the same thing. We can 'test' each method, 'probe' it and find what pleases us best.

Different feelings and emotions, captured in the moment, can help to bring out the different colours in your voice.

You could imagine that you are speaking to your very best friend. You want them to totally understand what and who you are. Be kind to yourself: you may not find the words you really need at the first take. If you were a professional speaker or singer you would often experience the pressure of 'trying to get it right': give yourself a bit of space.

Let's suggest some subject matter:

- Something that made you smile or laugh.

- Something somebody said that surprised you or excited you.

- Something that was special, that you want to remember for ever.

- A simple description of what is around you. This could be what you can hear (music playing, children shouting), what you can smell (supper cooking, roses blooming), or what you can see (dogs playing, cars moving).

- Something that moves you – music you love, a film you've seen, etc.

Focus on the **subject** of your talk; don't think about *how* you're going to tell your story. Each time you begin a new recording, just start to talk. If you don't like what you've said, if it 'comes out wrong', that's fine. It's your recording, no one else will hear anything you don't want them to hear. A professional performer would expect to get it 'wrong'; they would call it a 'rehearsal'.

'Once upon a time, there were three bears.' You probably know the next line? You could tell me the story. But if I rushed through it, slurring all the words together, 'Daddy bearmummybearandbabybear …' I bet you would not be pleased, because I wouldn't be showing proper respect for the story.

Are you tempted to rush through parts of your speech? 'I'll go through this bit quite quickly because most of you know it …' If they know it why are you telling them? If it's worth speaking at all it is worth speaking well. And they might 'know it', but perhaps they don't know it like *you* know it. They know the facts, but they don't know what you think or feel about the facts.

Take time to silently mouth your presentation text. Shape the words with your mouth. No whispering. Totally silent, except for the little clicking sounds you may hear when you make plosive consonant sounds like 'puh' or 'tuh'. It will bring you into real time rather than the time it takes to think through an idea. Brains are quick, but bodies are slow.

Evaluate how much time it takes to articulate your

thoughts clearly. Now speak the presentation out loud, and hear extra clarity, and perhaps a bit more passion.

Speak out loud

I am not convinced that watching yourself in the mirror is useful, though many would disagree with me. If you find it useful, then do it. Why am I not sure it's a good idea? I think it is all too easy to look at the wrong things – see spots on our noses that aren't there. If you saw yourself fidgeting around and moving from one foot to another then it could be useful to note. But watching yourself in the mirror could create a rather artificial situation, quite different from being in front of an audience. And it might divert your attention from other important things: why are you there? What is your task?

SPEAKING EXERCISE 1

Scientists tell us that we each have about twenty different notes in our voice, from the highest note to the lowest. We tend to use only four or five of these notes, and if we're nervous or anxious our vocal range is likely to get even smaller. So there could be a lot of 'uncharted territory' out there; vocal possibilities you've barely even dreamed of. Think of every different note in your voice as having a different colour. Wouldn't you like your voice to be more colourful?

To experience more of that colour we need first to relax the throat area.

Find a 'hot potato' space in your throat – the yawny space you might find if you were trying to eat a potato, and found it a little hotter than you'd bargained for. You would not want it to touch the sides of your throat, so you'd open up the space.

Sing on one single note the numbers one to five, then breathe in. Sing the numbers six to ten, and then breathe in. Sing eleven to fifteen, breathe in, and then sixteen to twenty.

Now, without stopping to think about it, SPEAK the numbers, breathing after every five as before. Put your hands on your ribs – can you feel them moving as you breathe? Keep the energy lifted and sustained right to the last sound of the last word.

SPEAKING EXERCISE 2

Find the same 'hot potato' space in your throat as before. Put your hands on your ribs and check you're breathing well.

Sing the numbers one to five on a rising note ↗. Simply start on a lower pitch and end on a higher pitch. Sing the next phrase, six to ten, on a falling note ↘. Start on the upper pitch and end on the lower, back where you started. Eleven to fifteen will glide up ↗, sixteen to twenty will glide back down ↘.

Take plenty of time to breathe between each phrase of numbers – don't rush. When you're done, SPEAK the numbers straight away. Having exercised your vocal range you should hear a bit more colour in your voice.

You can also try these exercises on your presentation text. Sing six short phrases of your text on the same note, and then immediately return to the beginning and speak the same phrases. Check that your ribs are moving freely, and that the good confident voice you should find when you sing is still strongly projected when you speak.

When you use Speaking Exercise 2 you will sing six phrases of your text, alternating the upward and downward glides, then immediately start to speak the same words. Give yourself time to breathe between phrases, and focus on projecting your story to the audience rather than on the pitch of your voice. You might want to record yourself, so that you can listen back to any changes in your delivery. As you've been introducing your voice to some new higher and lower notes, I hope you'll begin to hear new colours in your speaking. As with all of these exercises you might need a little time to get the best out of them.

Rehearsing with presentation material

Be clear about the sequence of events. You'll feel more confident if you run through the performance schedule in detail.

What happens first? Do we see a slide, then you start to speak, or do you start to speak then we see a slide? It sounds like a little thing, but if you want to control your time in front of the audience then you need to know what is happening. As you rehearse what you want to say, picture the whole scene. What is on the screen as you are speaking? When do you refer directly to what is on the screen?

What do I do with my hands?

We need to address anything that might make us feel less confident, and people can often get self-conscious about their hands while speaking. There is no perfect way to stand or sit or behave and what is appropriate will always relate to what feels comfortable to us in the situation. If you were having an argument with a friend, or telling someone you loved them, I bet you wouldn't be thinking about what to do with your hands. Why? Because something else would be more important. So let's see if we can use some exercises to help us to feel more at home in our bodies.

If our bodies are tense then any move could feel wrong; when our hands feel tense we get tempted to make movements that have nothing at all to do with what we are saying.

 This exercise can help you relax tension in the shoulders and arms and hands. I call it 'Windmills'. Stand up and imagine you have a big whiteboard, an arms-length out in front of you, and you want to draw a big circle on it. Stretch out one arm and draw the biggest circle possible on your imaginary board. Keep on drawing, and make the circle bigger. Draw the circle faster. Let your other arm join in. The two arms could circle in the same direction, or opposite directions. Enjoy the energy of your hands and arms and shoulders whizzing round. If you're in a really private space, and you're happy to make a noise then say 'ssssss' or sing 'zzzzzz' as your arms circle. Continue for about 30 or 40 seconds and then stop. I hope your arms feel tingly and alive?

Still making your arm circles, speak some of your presentation text for about one minute. Then do the same section of text again, standing still. You should feel the energy still there in your arms, and that should make you less self-conscious.

Now speak a minute of your presentation making really big gestures with your hands. Really emphasize each point you make. Then go back to the beginning and speak the same bit of the speech, standing still, though not rigid or frozen. Just believe that all the energy and power of what you want to say will come out in your voice. How does that feel and sound?

These exercises should make you feel that you have choices. On the day, you might want to move your hands or you might want to be still. If you are well-rehearsed, perhaps you could relax and trust yourself a bit.

Getting into gear

If you've been sitting at a computer for hours and then need to be vocally energetic you'll need to get into the right gear to bring yourself up to performance level. Your brain feels tired, your body feels sluggish. You need energizing, and another cup of coffee isn't the answer.

'Energy Builder' exercises can be done before or during a meeting or a presentation. They function like taking a vitamin pill or an energy-boosting drink, but I like to think they're more enjoyable.

ENERGY BUILDER 1

Imagine you're watching yourself moving around energetically. You could be running up and down some stairs, or swimming five lengths of a pool, or hitting a cricket ball, or riding a horse, or in the gym or climbing a mountain …

Stay with whichever fantasy you fancy for a minute. Then imagine the climax: you've done five laps of the stairs; the swimming pool is conquered; the ball is hit in a way that wins the game; the gym circuit is completed. You are out of breath, but very pleased with your performance. The fantasy must be something that encourages you to use all of your imagination, and you must surrender to it and allow it to take you, for a few moments, into a different world.

RESULT: Your energy lifts, you feel triumphant, you breathe more easily, and the ideas will flow.

ENERGY BUILDER 2

Have your notes or cue cards in front of you and pick a key word or phrase. Imagine the same energetic fantasy as before, and when you reach the climactic moment *silently shout* the word or phrase. To silently shout, imagine your favourite team have just scored the winning goal – you want to shout out loud but your wife has just got the baby off to sleep, and you have to express your excitement in total silence.

RESULT: When you come to speak that phrase it will be more dynamic and filled with action.

Q&A

Some clients love this part of their presentation, as they feel like their work is done and they can pass the baton to the audience. The responsibility is shared. In some cases you can even plan your whole presentation as question and answer, but you would need to provide the questions for yourself.

But others dislike Q&As, or at least find them irritating. You might feel that you've said all you want to say, and that if anyone has a question it's because they weren't listening in the first place. Why should you make the extra effort? Think about your function. Perhaps 'you' don't see why you should be bothered, but the person in your 'role' should feel differently. You might feel that people ask inappropriate or even plain silly questions – again think of the 'role'; it's your job to make sure they understand. You need to practise playing your part.

TRY IT NOW!

I call this exercise 'The Sandwich'. There are three sections, and you'll tell a story about something that happened in your life. The material that you present should last about three minutes, it should be short and to the point.

Your story needs to have a centre, like a sandwich. Just as you might choose tuna mayonnaise or paprika chicken as the main event in your sandwich, so here you need to think about what will fill the centre of your story.

Holidays are useful as subject matter, or you could tell us about how you got the job, or the first grandchild or the electric power drill that you'd always wanted. Perhaps you passed your driving test, or the mortgage offer finally came through or your team got through to the semi-final for the first time.

The top layer of the sandwich (the bread) will tell your audience why you wanted whatever it was, why you needed it and why it seemed like such a good idea. Then the middle section (the filling) is where it happens – you've got it, achieved it and are doing it. The bottom layer of sandwich (bread again) will tell us what happened next, and what the upshot is. What's it like now you've got what you want? Are you glad you did it? Or would you advise us not to do it, or to do it differently? What did you learn from it? Should we not buy a power drill?

So a 'Sandwich' story about your holiday could go something like this: The top layer is that you deserve a break – you plan and plan, it won't take too long to get there (so the brochure says …), etc. The filling of your story is the holiday itself: although the flight is delayed and they haven't quite finished building the hotel, you find great restaurants, learn a new Spanish dance you can't quite remember the name of and the sun shines non-stop. So overall it's a great success. The bottom layer of the sandwich is then that friends at work say you look ten years younger, and you've even managed to lose some weight after all that dancing. (Though you wouldn't recommend the hotel.)

THINK ABOUT IT

Practising presentations with a friend

If you have friends with similar concerns you could usefully join forces, and get some practice structuring and delivering a presentation or speech. You might find it useful to set down some ground rules about how you need your friend to critique you. What do you want to get out of this exercise? You might have presented material before and received specific comments. Do you shape your story clearly? Do you sound confident as you speak? Do you keep to the time frame you've given yourself, or do you sound rushed? You want the comments to be objective and precise; then you can go back to the drawing board, think about what you've learned, and deliver the material again. The best way to improve is to work in an atmosphere of constructive criticism. You might like to rehearse with your voice recorder as you decide on the material you're going to present.

Another useful aspect of this exercise is that you get to change roles. You do your presentation and receive a critique, then you get to critique your friend. We all learn very quickly that it is often far easier to tell someone else how to correct their mistakes than it is to correct our own. So while you want to give a clear and accurate judgement to your friend, remind yourself to show a little compassion. The first comment you make after hearing their presentation should be positive and contain some praise. Then tell them how to make it better.

---

9. Be prepared

Find out whatever you can about the venue as soon as you can. Think of it as a kind of performance space. Sometimes the space will be fixed. If you have any choice make sure you are in a good position to see and be seen, and to hear and to be heard.

If you are using extra presentation materials, think about your relationship to the screen, as many people as possible need to see both you and the screen without having to keep turning round. You need to see the audience, but you don't need to be facing the main screen if you have your own small screen or laptop directly in front of you. Keep reminding yourself that you are the main event, the screen is secondary. Make yourself available to the audience or it will be difficult to create and sustain a relationship with them. Find out who will be in charge of changing the slides.

If there is a choice I would opt for a clip-on microphone rather than a hand-held. Hand-held mikes, though perhaps more powerful, can be tricky to use. If you do have to use a hand-held mike, practising at home holding a hairbrush is not quite as daft as it sounds. The major 'trick' is that if your head moves to the right, then the mike needs to go to the right with you, or you will lose your amplification – this sounds obvious, but under pressure people often forget. The clip-on mike takes care of itself.

It's very tempting to think that the mike will do all the work for you, but it won't. If your voice is under-energized and colourless the mike may make it louder, but it will not make it more interesting or give it core energy, so speak at normal volume at least.

THINK ABOUT IT Could you give out notes after you speak rather than before? You want the audience focussing on you, not reading the manual. If you do need to hand something out before you speak, ask yourself: what do the audience need to see, and why?

The audience script

These are some of the ways that the hand-out – or the 'audience script' – you give to the audience before you begin to speak could work to your advantage:

- If the hand-out poses a question and you answer the question in your presentation.

- If the hand-out gives a series of statistics, and you explain what the statistics signify and why they are important.

- If the hand-out tells the part of the story that is best conveyed with a picture or a diagram, and you verbally join the dots together so that there is a clear shape.

Clients often tell me that they need to make full copies of their presentation available before the event, so that people unable to be there can access the material. So with that in mind, there are actually three different 'scripts' that need thinking about:

1. **The Full Script.** This version will include everything that those unable to attend would otherwise miss.

2. **The Audience Script.** The audience may like to have the full, written version but tell them only as much as will encourage them to be a good audience and focus on you.

3. **The Performer Script.** The performer would usually benefit from having their own script with just the notes needed to support confident delivery.

I know three scripts sounds like a lot of extra work, but the benefits could outweigh the effort.

 If you use notes, check where you can place them in the venue. Is there a table or lectern where you can easily access them? This is all part of 'setting the scene', making sure everything you need to feel confident is there so that you can concentrate on being with the audience.

PREPARATION EXERCISE 1

Before you enter the arena, we need to strike a balance between getting you energized and relaxed. You're probably sitting down, reading these words. Has the chair got a grudge against you? Could it be your friend instead, and support you? Enjoy the support and breathe deeply. Take time to centre yourself, and think about these three things as you breathe:

1. If your energy stays locked in your body you won't express yourself well.

2. Energy tends to get locked up in the joints of the body. We tighten up and freeze. Let your mind gently journey around your body, and visualize your energy flowing through all the joints: toes, ankles, knees, spine, elbows, shoulders, jaw …

3. If you imagine that your breath is flowing out to the four corners of the space – the furthest, the highest, the lowest parts – you are conquering that space. Actors do this when they are in a new theatre. Sometimes the space is so big and scary, but if you can feel like you own it you will act with confidence.

PREPARATION EXERCISE 2

The human body is not always easy to manage. We have two feet of not enormous size when we think of what they have to help to support: up to six feet and more of solid mass, with the head, the heaviest bit of the body for its size, on top. So it can sometimes be difficult to feel balanced and stable.

Stand up and focus on your feet. Imagine standing on a train with nowhere to sit and nothing to hold on to. Your feet will need to find a good contact with the floor – if the train is moving, the floor will be moving too. You need to keep the feet relaxed, so let them be quite soft and heavy and you'll be less likely to stumble or fall. The pay-off is that when you unlock your knees and soften your feet you will also unlock your breathing muscles. As we've looked at earlier, deep breathing can work wonders for your voice and help to keep you calm. By maintaining this strong but flexible connection with the ground you have put yourself in a good position to speak and perform with power and confidence.

Do you feel balanced between right and left? How much of each foot can you feel touching the floor? Visualize each foot as a kind of tripod. Big toe and little toe are the front two-thirds of the tripod. Your heel is the back of the tripod, the final third. Make sure some of the weight of the foot is balanced over your heel. You may feel the lower part of your back begin to stretch as you gently press down onto your heel for a few moments. This means your stomach muscles are free to move. Breathe deeply. Survey the space around you. You are the boss. This is your space. You have a right to be here.

I would strongly recommend that you actually practise this on a train or bus. If you can stay standing without panicking and grabbing hold of something, you've got it right!

Imagine you can see your breath. Out it goes, flying confidently across the space. And along comes the new breath: accept it; take time to let it fill you. No effort. Out and in, out and in. Why? Because otherwise your chattering mind will take over and tell you lots of scary lies. Breathing is good.

Find a focal point in front of you. It could be the first thing that catches your eye: a light switch, a coat-hook or whatever. Your breath flows out towards that focal point very smoothly. Taking its time. Imagine you want to touch that focal point with your breath, and keep touching until you need to breathe in. Breathe in gently. No gasps. No rushing. Send the new breath out. Same focal point, different focal point, it doesn't matter at all. Do five complete breath cycles. Don't you feel better?

Do this exercise before you enter the performance space. Nobody needs to know you're doing it. You can practise as many times you want, any time, any day. You don't need to puff and pant and strain. You are just doing a rather formalized version of something you've done as long as you've been alive.

Entering the space

As you walk into the building, or even as you walk into place to begin delivering your message, what would you like to hear? All the sounds of the world are at your disposal, as long as you can imagine them. Trumpets could sound, angels could sing. If this were a film, what kind of music would play to accompany the hero or heroine as they entered their finest moment? Hear that music in your head as you walk to your spot.

As you enter the performance space stand, or sit and stop for a moment, focus on what is supporting you, and let yourself be supported. And breathe. If you can calm yourself at the outset you'll be set up for the rest of your performance.

Beginnings

Start with single words and short phrases. 'Hello', 'good morning', 'thank you'. If you've got a mike and haven't had a chance to practise with it, you can 'test the water'. If people are looking blank at you perhaps they're not hearing you. If they've got hands over their ears you could probably quieten down a bit.

There is the greatest temptation to rush at the beginning of any talk. Presentations, meetings, first contact with new people in social situations. Remember that your partners in this situation probably feel just the same. They're suffering too! Just slow down and you'll calm not just yourself, but your audience too.

The performance dance: engaging with your audience

You engage the audience with your first move: a smile, a welcome, an introduction. You make it clear that you are there with them – centred in the space with them – breathing with them. And you want to share with them whatever your story is. You need to believe that they will offer you something in return: their ears, their eyes, their thoughts.

You begin the dance, you move a few steps; you inspire the audience to think/question/analyze/add two and two together. You give them time to digest, to add their energy to what you've given them. Then you teach them some more steps, add some more figures to the calculations they already have.

If you were in the audience, what would you like the person in front of you to do?

When you plan your introduction, don't spend too much energy defining the actual words you might use. Focus on what you are *doing*.

If I were in the audience I would want the speaker to want to greet me. 'Hello' or 'Hi' or 'Good morning'. Their desire to engage with me would be most important. So you might want to thank the audience for coming. You might want to thank them for asking you to come. There might be someone quite particular in the audience, or on a platform there with you, who had a major part in your being there.

I'd also want you to look at me as you addressed me. You might need to introduce yourself. You might want to thank someone else for introducing you. Engagement is key. Think about how you'd like to be spoken to, and try to match it.

I find it useful to keep each part of this beginning quite separate: the greeting, the introduction, the welcome. Breathe between each section, and listen to your audience.

Go through the whole speech or presentation and take out all the linking words that you really don't need. 'And's and 'but's and 'however's and 'therefore's. Leave only what is really necessary. In written language these links can be useful, but when you are taking part in a live event, your actually being there could be all the linking you need. Trim your text and you have more free space. For pausing. For breathing. And for getting your message across.

I might then want to know what you – a seemingly nice person who has welcomed me, thanked me and introduced yourself to me – are actually doing here. What have you come for? Are you talking about the price of cheese, or fish or what?

If in doubt, keep taking yourself into the audience. Show them by what you DO that you want to engage with them. You might want to educate them, amuse them, surprise them – or even frighten them! Or any other doing word you can think of.

At all times, you need to consider both what you *want* people to do (applaud/get up/sit down/look at something), and what you expect they *might* do (laugh/smile/applaud). How important is it whether or not they laugh/smile/applaud/stand up/sit down at certain points in the presentation?

A simple example: if you really want to know how many of your audience prefer sugar-free muesli then ask them to stand up or put their hands up. Give them a specific instruction. Otherwise they might simply not know how to react to your question, much as they might like to. And you would have an awkward moment, which make us nervous.

This is why actors will usually tell you that comedy is far harder to play than tragedy because you have to decide whether to wait for a laugh. If you carry on talking then you might stop the audience laughing. If you wait too long you might feel a bit unloved.

It might be nice if they laugh. But they may be laughing inside, without displaying it. You have more of your story to tell, so it's probably best to find a way to move on.

Imagine that somebody is asking you what your speech is about. What would you tell them? What are you talking about and why are you talking about it?

Taking no more than one minute, speak out loud and give a complete overview of your speech. Clearly state, in brief, how you will begin and end, and what comes in the middle. When you actually do the presentation, you will remember your own calm voice telling you exactly why you need to speak and it will give you confidence.

As someone who has done a lot of performing, sometimes eight shows a week for months on end, I can confess to you that even for seasoned actors something always goes 'wrong'. And I'm telling you this to encourage you, as more often than not nobody notices but you. If you did decide to repeat the bit you got 'wrong' in order to try and get it 'right' the audience would not thank you because they want you to get on with the story. And perhaps most importantly, sometimes when it goes 'wrong' you actually find a better way to tell your story. It can be as if some instinct is kicking in that tells you to say it this way rather than that way. Human beings are not robots, and in the heat of the moment that humanity might mean everything does not go according to plan. But as long as you remember to breathe all will be well.

And if you feel your knees shaking, and it worries you, just think back to when you were watching someone else do a presentation. How much time did you spend looking at their knees?

PART THREE
Speeches for specific events

So far, we have been talking about ideas and techniques that you can use for all sorts of situations, including speaking in a meeting as well as doing a presentation. We've also looked at general rules regarding decisions about content and delivery of your message. But now I think we should look at some more specific examples of public speaking.

10. The wedding speech

I'm sure many of you have promised to do a wedding speech, and then when you've had more time to think about it have begun to feel the fear. You might have wondered how on earth you could even begin to plan what you're going to say, never mind come through the event itself unscathed. You are not alone, I promise you.

This is such a personal day. The day of all days for the couple involved, and their families. So I want to offer you some structures and ideas on how to generate material, gather your thoughts and make plans. Most importantly, I will show you how to have everything in place so you feel supported and confident when you come to the moment of delivery.

You'll be tempted to search the internet for the 'perfect' content for your speech – there are more than enough suggestions about what you should and should not say or do. Many could be helpful. But – and call me old-fashioned on this one – don't forget to search your own heart, even though it will take time and energy, and faith that you have something worthwhile to say.

Depending on how formal the wedding will be, if there are a number of people making speeches you'll need to decide who makes the toasts. It is better to check on this. Though, on the face of it, most of us don't really mind being thanked – or drunk to – twice. But sometimes there are protocols and procedures. So much time and money goes into the day, it's best to know what the structure is so that you can work within it. Here are some of the basics to bear in mind.

Length of the speech

This is an easy one. Most people seem to agree that between five and seven minutes is about right. It could depend on how many speeches there are. More than the usual three – father of the bride, groom, best man – and you might want to cut down the length accordingly.

Function of the speech

Before we start to focus on what you're going to say, let's see if you can answer some basic questions. Why me? What am I supposed to be talking about? What is my talk supposed to achieve? Who am I speaking for? Is this a purely personal comment, or am I speaking on behalf of others?

On any kind of formal occasion formal things might need to be said. We can think in terms of **role play**. Bride, groom, father of the bride and best man are all roles that people take on for that specific occasion. We need to make sure you explore and confidently find your best way to play your part. It can be hard for any actor asked to play Hamlet, as so many others have already played him. But, equally, no one will play the part like you will play it, because you are unique.

THINK ABOUT IT

What about jokes?

I don't know about you, but if anyone announces that they are going to tell me a 'really funny' story or a joke my laughter can easily dry up altogether. When we try to be funny, most of us end up being anything but. There is something in the trying that runs counter to true humour. And at a wedding you have to be doubly careful you don't offend anyone.

Make it personal

'Not a lot of people know that …' is a very good line. And we all love a secret, don't we? (Even if it is being shared with the million others in the audience.)

REMEMBER THIS!!!

'Do you remember that time? That really hot day. You were swimming naked in the river. I hid your clothes …'

Ask yourself the question: did he or she really see the funny side of that? The principal players on this occasion should be honoured and given due respect. Both them, and their nearest and dearest. If in doubt, go for a story where the person you are talking about ended up laughing. Or got their own back! Anything you think might upset those with sensitive natures, leave out.

Balance the facts and feelings

Sometimes telling a very personal story by focussing on the facts can best display how emotional we feel. I recently watched a US TV drama where a young man was speaking at the funeral of his grandmother. After his parents were killed in a car crash his grandmother gave him a home. He was only ten, and the first night he wet the bed. She got him cleaned up and let him share her own bed, telling him that it would be better if he didn't wet the bed again or they would run out of clean sheets. We got – from the script-writers, and the good acting – a fine balance between tears and laughter. We could understand from that one short story just how much the grandmother meant to him, even though he spoke in a very simple, unemotional way.

Don't be afraid to introduce yourself

I know that if we see the bride on your arm entering the church we might put two and two together. But you may not be the bride's father. You might be her uncle or another family friend. I think we listen better if we know who we are listening to, so don't be afraid to introduce yourself.

Don't drink and drive

I know that I'm going to sound like a killjoy, but drinking and performing don't go together, I believe. You may well be tempted – and friends may encourage you – to 'relax' yourself with a little drink. It will always be debatable but I think there is good evidence that alcohol and control are not good companions. You can make up for it later if you like.

I once worked with a woman called Joan, who needed to give a speech at her daughter's wedding. The daughter's relationship with her father had, sadly, been a rather distant one, and she had been saying for a number of years: 'Mum, when I get married, you're going to have to do the Father-of-the-Bride speech.' So what were the concerns that Joan had to face, and how did she find solutions? Joan was not used to public speaking, and she was not at all confident that she could make a successful speech. She was also only too aware that it is more usual for the bride's father to speak. She really feared she might feel out of place, and that people would not know who she was. What spurred her on was her promise to the daughter she loved, and that there really was no other candidate for the job.

Joan needed to make some decisions about the content. She had a wealth of stories about her daughter, so she wasn't short of material, and we decided that she would plan for a speech of no more than five minutes. I persuaded Joan to try recording her thoughts and ideas and though she certainly wasn't used to the sound of her own voice as soon as she started telling her stories she forgot to be self-conscious.

We planned the first section of the speech, the introduction, very carefully as this was the part Joan wanted to feel extra secure about. She naturally wanted to greet everyone – there were lots of people she didn't know, and she felt strongly that the large guest list was a credit to her successful daughter. She wanted to introduce herself, and to make it absolutely clear how she felt about standing there. 'As April's mum,' she decided she wanted to say, 'I'm extra proud to be doing this speech.' She wanted everyone to feel very welcome, so that was added to the list of contents for the first section. 'Greet, introduce, welcome' would be a shorthand version for what Joan was going to do.

Joan chose three simple, family-oriented stories to tell the audience about April. She didn't want to sound over-emotional, and decided after listening to her audio recordings that she liked the simplest versions of the stories best. The stories included grandparents, family holidays and when April's new husband had first visited their family home. She found it very useful taking all the unnecessary 'and's and 'but's and other linking words out of her script, because it helped her to come across in the clearest and most confident way. And she had her speech printed on cue cards that she could comfortably hold in her hands.

Joan's voice was perfectly clear and her only fear was that the nerves would stop her breathing deeply and make her voice a bit shaky. We looked at how she would stand, knees relaxed and feet feeling soft and heavy, and as we rehearsed the speech we made sure there was ample time to pause and allow the audience a few moments to enjoy the stories.

Joan was overjoyed at the outcome and she wrote me

a lovely email after the wedding. Her daughter's boss had been there at the wedding and she'd said it was one of the best wedding speeches she'd ever heard. The bride cried, and asked for a copy of the speech so she could put it in her 'treasure' box!

'Desperate needs' will sometimes lead to 'desperate deeds'. That's the saying. Joan would not for the world have wanted to disappoint her daughter. She would not for one second have thought that she had any skill as a speech giver, but by working out what she, uniquely, could bring to the situation, she was able to be a resounding success.

How do I decide what I'm going to say?

Now that we've looked at some general ideas about basic structures and subjects best to avoid, we need to get you focussing on the material that you might like to use in your speech. This next exercise will help you do just that.

WRITING EXERCISE 1

Get out your voice recorder and simply start to talk about the wedding, the couple, and anything related that springs to mind. It may seem a little crazy at first, but you'll get used to it. Why are you talking to yourself? Because you want to find out what you have to say. Tell yourself anything and everything. How thrilled you are, how scared you are. What do you know? Where do you need to do a bit of research? If you've done a similar speech before and it wasn't the success you had hoped for, ask yourself why. Perhaps you didn't plan enough? Perhaps you didn't practise enough? Well now you're taking care of that. Remind yourself of your relationship to the bride and groom, how long you've known them, the simple but emotional facts of the times you've spent together.

Focus on what you are thankful for. What are you grateful for? What brings a smile to your face – it could just bring a smile to the face of others. What do you wish for? What do you hope for? Health, wealth, and happiness are not a bad little trio. (And wealth doesn't always mean having money in the bank.)

What is most welcome and exciting about this new beginning, this new partnership? If you are the father of the bride, how do you feel about this new member of the family? The old image of 'not losing a daughter, but gaining a son' can still ring true.

When you listen back, you should hear gaps between words and phrases that let you know where you might put in commas and full stops if you were working these ideas into your speech. Try writing out some ideas, either with punctuation, or just leaving gaps between the different phrases. You want your script to clearly show you where one idea ends and a new one begins.

Eating and digestion are useful analogies. I invite you to dinner. I give you a first course: some soup. You enjoy it. Do you want me to grab the soup bowl away as soon as you've had the last mouthful and place the next course in front of you? Wouldn't you like to sit a moment and enjoy the lingering taste of the food you've eaten? Similarly, if you are giving your audience a greeting, a personal moment you have designed just for them, might they not want a moment to savour it?

Now we're going to look at what might make suitable material for each member of the speech-making party. Remember, while we're talking specifically about a wedding here, many of the lessons in this chapter are equally applicable to other situations.

The father of the bride

This is a very simple example of a father of the bride's speech.

As in the cue cards that we looked at earlier, the left-hand column reminds you of what you are doing and the right-hand column suggests how you might do it.

Greet	Good evening
Welcome	I'm so very pleased you can all be here to share Lucy and Sean's wedding day
Introduce yourself	As Lucy's father it's my proud duty to give this speech I've already 'given her away' that was the hard bit The rest of the day is pure pleasure

Beginnings	All good stories begin at the beginning so we're told And I was there when Lucy was born Not a lot of comfort to Lucy's mother I'm sure I'd read somewhere Winston Churchill was quoted as saying That all babies looked like him I thought he was joking I think she's improved a bit since then don't you Sean?
Schooldays	Lucy loved going to school Always first up in the morning And I found a picture of her we've had it blown up so you can all see you thought it was lost didn't you Lucy In a school concert Gilbert & Sullivan a fairy in *Iolanthe* Count yourself lucky I was going to show them that one of you in your Goth phase Sean hasn't seen that one either I don't think we ever got all of that black hair dye off the bathroom washbasin

University and beyond	My darling daughter I have joked with you enough I shall now embarrass you with sentimentality Or embarrass myself I did cry when you left home to go to university Your mother almost despaired of me And yes I did cry at your university graduation I know I said it was my contact lens And I shall probably have a little weep when we get home tonight
The husband	Sean I've watched your relationship with Lucy develop I've seen your love grow And I am a happy man today I know you'll take care of her if she'll let you she can be stubborn I've seen your patience one word of advice don't let her drag you out on too many shopping trips that will wear you out take it from one who knows

The toast	I want to wish you both much happiness from me and from Lucy's mother Diana
	Ladies and Gentlemen will you join me and raise your glasses
	To Lucy and Sean the bride and groom

The groom

It is often said that of all the speech-givers on the wedding day the groom will be 'forgiven' almost anything. After all it's not really the most important part of his day. But you will want to do yourself, and the occasion, and especially your new wife, proud.

You should have been speaking your initial ideas into a voice recorder. Listening back you will, I hope, hear yourself chatting, having what sounds like a conversation. Not lecturing. Not monologuing.

The bridegroom will very often speak directly after his new father-in-law. This is your first moment, and first moments are important. I want you to enjoy it. I want you to give yourself plenty of time. So listen back to the phrases you've recorded and divide the text up into small parts. I'll use a 'dummy' version I've written below to give you some ideas about scripting and structuring.

Thank you for your kind words   Michael

And of course   I totally agree with everything
   you said
Thank you   for entrusting   Lucy   to me
your beautiful daughter is now   my beautiful
   wife   I am so proud

This is pretty generic. It's probably a good thing to (at least) start off agreeing with your new in-laws. And beauty and pride are good things to celebrate at a wedding. Don't be afraid of the simplicity of words. Choice of words is important, but most important is that you are speaking from your heart. And I'm going to use the word 'respect' too. For each of the speakers, find what you can respect and honour. Aim to bring concord.

Now, if these were your chosen words, you would practise speaking them out loud. You would have listened back to your recorder and found the kind of phrasing that most suited you. How do you feel best, speaking what you want to speak? As long as you're not rushing through, I'm with you all the way.

We could have:

Thank you   Michael   for your kind words
And   I totally agree   of course   with
   everything you said

My next suggestion is that you use some shading to – as my computer describes it – 'colour the background behind the text or paragraph'. If you were writing long-hand rather than using a computer you could put a different-coloured line down the side of each section. As we continue thinking through material for this speech, we will be writing it out word-for-word.

Why am I suggesting this? I think it can be a good way to begin. After you've used this technique you may decide you prefer another version, but if you look at the whole script, and it is divided into coloured sections, it will be easier to see the journey of your thoughts from beginning to end. It can also act as a prompt, reminding you that when you get to the end of each section it's time to stop, breathe, refocus. Time for your audience to do a bit of metaphorical chewing and swallowing and digesting.

We could divide our groom's speech into sections straight away. You will see three columns on the page, as you did with 'The Motorway' technique we used in chapter seven, but this is a different exercise. We are not for the moment considering exactly *what* you will say, that comes later. For now you need to decide *who* you are talking to, *what* you are doing when you speak to them (perhaps you need to introduce them to others, or thank them, or praise them) and *why* you feel you'd like to do that (they've been especially helpful or kind or done beautiful flower arrangements). Once you have made decisions about these three things, then you can decide on the words you want to use. And remember, sometimes the short version of the story will be more powerful and memorable than the long one.

WHO ARE YOU TALKING TO?	WHAT ARE YOU DOING?	WHY ARE YOU DOING IT?
Section one Dad-in-law	Thanking	Because you will presume that he will say something nice about his daughter. You will hope that he says something nice about you.

And it's pretty safe to say 'thanks for giving me your daughter's hand.' |
| **Section two** Everyone | Thanking Toasting | People have made an effort and travelled long distances.

Many would think it's not much of a wedding without those you care about being there to take part.

A toast to absent friends can include those who have sadly passed, but for you and your wife they are still very much part of your life. |
| **Section three** Readers/ Singers | Introducing Thanking Praising Storytelling | The congregation may not know them. It's interesting to know why you chose the performer, the piece. You are being the perfect host, helping people to get to know each other. |
| **Section four** Parents-in-law | Thanking Introducing Storytelling | They are letting you into the family.

Focus on anything you like about them – any kindness: be thankful for any help offered, financial or otherwise.

You may want to compliment the staff and service at your wedding reception venue. |

WHO ARE YOU TALKING TO?	WHAT ARE YOU DOING?	WHY ARE YOU DOING IT?
Section five Groom's parents	Thanking Introducing Storytelling Gift giving	Life is a journey. Someone will have been with you on that journey. Now you're married. Be sentimental, why not? Give thanks that you've never quite found the time and place to give before. And it is customary to say 'thank you' on behalf of your new bride: she has been allowed to marry you! Tell stories that could bring a smile to your parents' faces.

Sometimes gifts are given to both sets of parents, or just to both mothers. |
| **Section six** Best man | Thanking Storytelling | The traditional position is that the best man is somehow going to find a way to reveal secrets or otherwise embarrass the groom.

Tradition therefore might encourage the groom to have ammunition with which to counter the blows. And to get some blows of his own in before the best man gets to speak.

How the best man has performed his duties so far – today and at the stag night – will colour your feelings towards him at this moment. You may choose to tell your guests something about your friendship. |

WHO ARE YOU TALKING TO?	WHAT ARE YOU DOING?	WHY ARE YOU DOING IT?
Section seven Wife	Thanking Praising Storytelling	Favourite section: The wife. You might want to simply wax lyrical about love at first sight and perfection from day one. Some grooms like to remind their wife just what did happen at that first meeting. You are obviously a lucky man: she is beautiful: the world is perfect.
Section eight Bridesmaids	Thanking Praising Gifting Toasting	Bridesmaids are always lovely and kind and they probably have had a large part in creating the perfect wedding scene. Be grateful. But have a little fun with them if you like.

We have the sections, so now we need to look at what we want to *do* within each section. There is an acting exercise which a good friend of mine, a stage director, used to use. It's rather grand title was the 'I Want You to Know' game. It was especially useful for actors who have only two or three tiny scenes in each three-hour performance where they have memorable lines like, 'Your carriage awaits my lord,' or 'Your wife is waiting in the drawing room.' So for that second line the actor could devise a whole extra scene that would never be known to anyone but himself. It would go something like this:

I want you to know that I know you said not to come in because you were in a very important meeting. And it really is very cold out there in the corridor. Which is, by the way, the only place I'm allowed to sit. And you probably don't know, or care, that I didn't get any supper, as we got back late from your last meeting, and the cook had gone home. And I was just managing to have a bit of a snooze when there was this banging at the door and lots of shouting. And **your wife is waiting in the drawing room**.

Of course he is only allowed to say the line given in the text. But he can think and imagine his way through the preamble. The actor would hope the line would come over as more meaningful as a result of having psyched himself up. We cannot speak every word we think. We wouldn't want to. Some things are better left unsaid. But if we don't consider some of the thoughts that might usefully flow between our words, we might come over as being rather dull.

So with that in mind, let's return to the beginning of our speech. This time I'll put the words to be spoken in bold, and some initial and connecting thoughts in regular type.

goodness dad-in-law for just one minute I thought
    you might really like me   only kidding
Thank you for your kind words   and I don't
    have to call you Mr Smith anymore   **Michael**
isn't she lovely my lovely wife you are so right
    telling me how lucky I am I know it I know it

And of course I totally agree with everything you said I am so lucky

Thank you thank you thank you thank you **for entrusting Lucy** my Lucy **to me**

just think we are really married and she does look so stunning so beautiful

Your beautiful daughter is now and I am going to say it **my beautiful wife** my beautiful wife I am so proud **I am so proud**

Speak the whole of that section out loud, including the connecting thoughts (you can use your own speech if you'd prefer). Then go back to the beginning and speak only the text in bold. You need to practise hearing your voice, speaking out, not muttering or mumbling. You could try recording it, so you have the chance to listen back. Now you've worked with the idea of including connecting thoughts I hope you hear that your speech sounds more confident?

Silence can make us a bit nervous, as on the whole we feel more able to judge how a situation is going when people are making noises. But you need to think of it this way: your guests will sit in silence and look at you in expectation because you are a star player and they want to give you all their attention.

Each wedding day is unique, and you want to find your unique style and content for the day.

This is the rest of my 'dummy' groom speech, written with built-in pauses. It may bear a resemblance to a wedding speech you have heard/written/spoken in the past, dear reader – it would be hard to come up with a wedding speech that did not have a plagiarized word or two somewhere within.

This wonderful day   would not be half as
    wonderful   without everyone being here
And I know   that mountains have been
    climbed   and rivers have been crossed
in the amount of effort   that many of you   have
    put into   getting here today
On behalf of my wife and I   I've been waiting to
    say that   my wife and I
I want to say a big big   thank you
There are some people   who are unable   to be
    here with us   in person
I know they are thinking of us   that we are in their
    hearts   and they are in our hearts too
Can we take a moment   to remember   and
    drink a toast   to absent friends

I'd like to introduce you to our
    readers   Mark   and Luca
Mark   was at university with Lucy

Luca and I   go back to junior school days
Lucy and I both love music and poetry   it felt
    really right   for both of us
That our kind   and talented friends   should be
    asked   to take part
Thank you for sharing your voices with us

Parents-in-law   I'd like to thank you
Diana   without your strong guiding spirit   and
    great common sense   I don't think   with all
    respect to my lovely wife   that either   the
    wedding dress   or the menus
for this splendid meal   would ever have been
    finally decided on
Those of you who have ever gone   on a
    shopping trip with Lucy   know that the
    day   will not end   before every shop   has
    been visited
Michael   your enormous generosity
has made it possible to have our wedding
    here   in this magnificent setting
I thoroughly enjoy   spending time   with both
    of you
I knew that marrying Lucy   would mean
    marrying   her family
And I   could not be happier

My mum and dad   have been the finest supports
    to me   that any boy could wish for
And I know I'm supposed to be a grown-up
    now   on my wedding day
But   every new adventure in my life   from
    changes of school   to first day at university
Has been punctuated   with my parents' good
    wishes   and a little more pocket money
By the way mum … (*look in wallet for money that is
    not there*)   oh I can catch you later
Your hearts were opened to Lucy   at that first
    meeting   I knew   that you knew
that she was the one
Oh goodness   perhaps we're all going to blub now

But onto more serious things   Lucy wanted me to
    thank you
for producing such a fine specimen   of perfect
    manhood
that was what you said   darling   wasn't it?

My best man   is my brother   not sure I made
    the right move there   Patrick
Until I hear the speech
And see what you've been carrying around   in
    the suitcase   all day
And yes   I know I wasn't supposed to see

You've been a great brother to me   over the
    years   Pat
I'm proud of you   and we don't want to spoil
    that   do we?
And don't forget   I've got two more best
    men   waiting in the wings   an heir and a
    spare
And they're on my side   or that was the
    idea   when I 'booked' them
I can rely on you chaps   can't I?
Martin and Gus   ladies and gentlemen   thank
    you both so much
except for that incident on the stag night   which I
    certainly don't want to dwell on

I've made my promises to Lucy today
My beautiful wife
There are a thousand reasons   why I am so
    proud   to be standing here today
a thousand reasons   why I love you
Lucy
It's five years since we met
I remember the day   I remember what you
    wore   I remember how you completely
    ignored me   well not ignored me   but spent
    more time with my brother   said he looked a
    bit like Prince William   which is a joke

But I won you round   and I have got a better
    head of hair than William
which must count for something   I should shut up
    now
Except that I could talk about you all day
The joy and great good humour   with which
    you   not only fill your own life
But the lives of all those who come into contact
    with you
You have made such an amazing difference to my life
You have given me your love
Everything I have   I give to you   I want to
    be   by your side   for the rest of our lives

I'm going to end by saying   thank you   to our
    lovely bridesmaids
Lucy's sister Eleanor   and   my sister Laura
You look lovely   you know you do   sit there and
    be embarrassed
I know you'll make me pay for it later
I'm right aren't I   everyone?
Seriously   you've done a fantastic job   and
    those dresses!
In fact I'm going to ask you to get up   Lucy and I
    have a little gift for each of you

Ladies and Gentlemen   will you all join me   and
    drink a toast   to Eleanor   and Laura

You might decide that you don't want a word-for-word script. You might feel that it would be better if you had no script with you at all. But I would rather see someone standing there with a whole book full of notes, if it gave them confidence. As long as the notes are just used as a reminder and support, not to be stared at throughout. Much worse would be watching someone struggling, trying to remember all the things that had been quite clear when they weren't in the limelight.

The next way you could write your speech down would be as an abridged version. These would be my suggestions, for my groom's speech. You will not know if the shortened text gives you enough support – if it will offer you a cue for everything that you need to say – until you rehearse with it. Then you can decide if you need more words, or fewer words, or just different words. But at the very least, I would advise you to leave any specific information in. Names, facts and figures can be the first things to slip one's mind.

Introduce readers   Mark   Luca
Mark University Lucy
Luca   junior school with me
we love music/poetry   felt right
kind talented friends
Thank you   for sharing
Parents-in-law   thank you
Diana   strong guide   common sense
    wedding dress chosen   menus decided on

shopping trips with Lucy   every shop   visited
Michael   generosity   made wedding here possible
I enjoy time with you
marrying Lucy   marrying family   totally happy

I think you get the idea.

The best man

The other two speeches may quite naturally focus on the bride. The best man will redress the balance. By tradition, the best man may need to do anything from helping the groom to capture his future bride from an enemy tribe and stopping her parents from capturing her back, to guiding the groom through his wedding night duties. But I am presuming most of these duties are a thing of the past!

You might need to research the parts of the groom's life that you are not well-acquainted with. And you do need to talk about the bride as well as the groom, even though you might know him far better than you know her.

Of all the speech-givers you should accept that it may be best to keep some things under wraps – ex-girlfriends, exact amount of beer enjoyed on the stag night (etc.) really are better left unspoken on this day. I have had this conversation more than once: 'So you'd cut that bit would you?' 'Well yes I would really …' 'You don't think it's funny?' 'I'm not sure the audience would appreciate it.' 'His rugby-playing mates will be there!' 'Yes, but so will his Gran. So you tell me.'

Everyone who does a speech will have a function according to his or her role. Dad or Mum will talk about their daughter. The groom will talk about his bride. You will talk about the groom, and saying something about the history of the man and how he comes to be making this commitment today will be expected.

 Get out that voice recorder. Start talking about any facts you know or can find. How long have the bride and groom been together? How long have they known each other? How did they meet? Some general biography of the bride will be useful to mix in with the bio of the groom. How has the groom changed since they got together?

What are their hopes and dreams? How did you meet the groom? Dad or Mum can tell us about the bride's schooldays, what can you tell us about the groom? Tell us about your friendship – with the groom and with the bride. Describe his personality. Talk about his achievements. Many people at a wedding don't really know as much about the main participants as we might imagine. Visualize the couple in a year's time. Five years' time.

There should be stories. And yes, it is accepted practice that some fun is had at the groom's expense. And that photos of naked babies on goatskin rugs might be exhibited. But talk from a loving heart.

If you are the best man it is key that you introduce yourself. It's traditional to thank whoever is hosting the reception – most usually the bride's parents. But the groom may already have done this, so best to check. If the groom has toasted the bridesmaids it is traditional for the best man to respond to the toast on their behalf: this can simply mean that you say 'thank you'.

Do consider the personality of the groom and the bride. What do you imagine that they would like you to say? It can be customary to end with another toast to the bride and groom. Here's a best man's speech I've written, coving all of these areas and using the techniques we've covered so far in the book:

Ladies and gentleman   good evening
For those of you who don't know me   my name
   is Patrick
Yes   I'm the little brother   but   for today at
   least   I'm the best man
There is a tradition of course   to choose your
   brother to be best man
Prince William   chose Prince Harry   and that
   seemed to turn out OK

Some men   choose their brother   so the story
   goes   because they think it's a safe bet
I mean a brother would only say the most
   complimentary things   wouldn't he?

Stands to reason   we shall see   brother of
    mine   we shall see

And yes   I think Lucy did have a bit of a soft spot
    for me   first of all at least

It doesn't come too easily   to tell your kid
    sister   that she looks nice
But   as best man   it is my happy duty   on
    behalf of the beautiful bridesmaids
our Laura   and Eleanor   to thank my
    brother   for his kind words
Well said brother

The internet is so useful   isn't it?
This is part of 'Advice to Brothers Acting as Best
    Man'
Be prepared for morning suit emergencies   safety
    pins   or even a stapler will always come in
    handy   now you know what I've got in the
    suitcase
More advice   nothing matters in comparison to
    one major thing
keep the groom alive for the wedding   there
    you see   I'm not a total failure

If I've always been known as the handsome
    one   you did say that mum   didn't you?

Sean was always the clever one   passed all his
    exams   got into the first choice university
I did miss him when he went off to Durham
although I was allowed to take over the biggest
    bedroom

I've always looked up to Sean   well   until I got
    to be taller than him
And yes I am   a little bit
Seriously it's not difficult to look up to Sean
Even as his brother   I can see so much to admire

There were girlfriends before Lucy   none lasted
    more than five minutes
I think Lucy was the first one to actually get asked
    out on a second date

He's a planner   my brother
Even when we were both at school   pocket
    money   and Saturday job wages would all be
    squirrelled away
if he wanted something   for his bike   CDs   his
    first iPod   everything was planned for

When we went on holiday   our sister Laura and
    I   would be finding ways to spend our pocket
    money   when we were hardly out of the car
but not Sean   plans had to be made

so many ice creams could be bought   each
    day   and no more

So I think   Lucy   that plans were made   quite
    soon after you and he met
Once you'd decided   that I was not quite right
    for you
Sean had today in his sights

Sport has always played a massive part in Sean's
    life
Sport and music
No one else in the family knows a B-flat from an
    F-sharp.

Sean and I both had piano lessons with the same
    teacher
Those were the days when everyone was Mr Mrs or
    Miss
Mrs Dawson was our teacher   I don't think she
    had a first name

She wasn't horrid or anything   but she knew I had
    no talent
I was at an age   when I wanted to be like my
    older brother
He wanted to play the piano   so I wanted to play
    the piano

And at the end of every term   we had to do this
    little concert
Parents were allowed in   and mum and dad
    usually came   though I begged them not to
They wanted to hear Sean   of course

One concert day   neither of our parents could
    come   and I knew they wouldn't be there
I'd practised even less than usual   I never
    seemed to get any better anyway
We all sat in her little hallway   waiting
the concert was in her sitting room   where the
    grand piano was
and I was getting paler and paler   as my turn got
    closer

and Sean   mum and dad don't listen to this bit
and Sean   cornered Mrs Dawson   and I heard
    them whispering

then he came up to me   'Mrs Dawson says you
    can go home'
I was speechless   'as you hurt your hand playing
    cricket
and you're worried you won't play well'
'I didn't …'   I started to say   'Go home,' said
    Sean.

I didn't go straight home   I hung around outside
   the house
so Sean and I could arrive home together

He wouldn't talk about it
That's Sean really   he knew how worried I
   was   about the playing
And though it was totally my fault   for not
   practising   he took care of it
He took care of me

And he'll take care of you Lucy

You'll take care of each other   I know

He may not be as handsome as me
But he's got a handsome heart

Sean and Lucy
I am very privileged   to be in your lives
I am honoured   to be playing this part in your
   wedding celebrations

Everyone here   your family   and all your friends
wish you a very happy and long life together

I'm going to propose a toast   Ladies and
   gentlemen

If you will be upstanding
Please raise your glasses   to toast the happy
   couple

Sean and Lucy

These techniques and ideas can be used to help you plan and prepare and rehearse for any number of events, especially ones that are family-oriented such as birthday parties or memorial services or funerals.

The job of doing a eulogy might go to someone just outside the main family circle, as especially at the funeral itself, those most directly affected could fear they would break down if they tried to voice their feelings, and would prefer someone else to speak their thoughts. This is a terribly sensitive job, and if you can find a way to touch on the triumphs and most memorable qualities of a person you will be of great comfort. You don't need to speak in an over-emotional way, just to tell how much someone was loved and appreciated.

At a memorial it could be appropriate to speak of some of the more light-hearted episodes from the life you are remembering. But as with the wedding speeches, these are very individual circumstances and you should seek advice from those most closely concerned, to find out what they would like to be said and shared.

Birthday speeches, for example, will encourage you to play the detective. There was a long-running TV show called *This is Your Life*, where long, lost friends suddenly popped up from far-flung places and the 'do you remember when' stories were shared. Whatever the situation, so much joy can be given if the right words are confidently spoken. Everyone has stories that should not be forgotten.

11. Doing a reading

There are many occasions where you may be asked to read a poem or other piece of text. This time the decision regarding 'what to say' is not yours, which could feel like a blessing, but can also be a curse. You can't change the bits you don't like or that don't feel quite right. I've spent a good part of my teaching career working on Shakespeare and, 'Can't we put it into our own words?' is often the request. The answer is, 'Yes, if it helps you to understand the text better', but eventually we need to return to what the man himself wrote.

Here are some ideas to work with. First, as with the task of generating your own text, speak it out loud. Don't be afraid, it won't bite you. And you may find, straight away, that you understand more when you hear the words than you did reading them silently in your head. A lot of poetry is built to be spoken, to be heard. Some of the meaning could be clearer because you hear the rhythm of the words, and some meaning may be stronger when you hear that certain words or phrases are repeated.

Let's take our first poem, 'To my Dear and Loving Husband', by Anne Bradstreet. Anne Bradstreet was the first woman writer to be published in the British North American colonies, so we are told, and this poem was written over 400 years ago, when she moved from her English home in

Northampton to America. It is, incidentally, a very popular poem at weddings.

Don't sit and think about it, read the whole poem out loud. Trip over words. Stumble and stutter. Mispronounce. Who cares? You are rehearsing. Rehearsals are where you are allowed to get it wrong. And how could you be expected to get it right when you've only just seen the text? You need to get to know it. Give yourself a break.

COMPREHENSION EXERCISE 1

'To my Dear and Loving Husband', by Anne Bradstreet

If ever two were one, then surely we.
If ever man were lov'd by wife, then thee.
If ever wife was happy in a man,
Compare with me, ye women, if you can.
I prize thy love more than whole Mines of gold
Or all the riches that the East doth hold.
My love is such that Rivers cannot quench,
Nor ought but love from thee give recompense.
Thy love is such I can no way repay.
The heavens reward thee manifold, I pray.
Then while we live, in love let's so persevere
That when we live no more, we may live ever.

As we did with part of my dummy bridegroom speech, it will be useful to explore what the character speaking these words might be thinking between the spoken phrases. The speaker in this poem is the wife talking to her husband. And we might imagine there is also a chorus of married women, listening in. Our speaker might even sound as if she's boasting, 'Go on, you try and tell me your husband is even half or a quarter as good as my husband!' She's talking about something that is deeply emotional to her, so we need to imagine that we feel like she does. Then our speaking will be very powerful.

I would advise you to write or type out your poem. You'll find that it somehow becomes more 'yours'. You know you did not actually write it, in a literal sense, but you are physically involved in transcribing the text, and that can make a big difference. You could imagine some connecting thoughts, and write them out, between the phrases of the text. Here are some suggestions for this poem.

> **If ever two were one** and goodness knows that's
>   what marriage is isn't it **then surely we** are
> **If ever man were lov'd by wife** and we hope that
>   lots of women love their husbands **then thee**
>   yes you are loved
> **If ever wife was happy in a man** and of course
>   I trust that lots of women are happy with their
>   husband

Compare with me come on just you try to
compare yourself **ye women** if you can   bet
you can't

I prize thy love how much do I value you do you
think? **more than whole Mines of gold** yes that
much

Or all the riches yes even richer than the goldmines
that the East doth hold and that is a lot

My love is such my love for you is so strong **that
Rivers cannot quench** nothing can cool the heat
of it

Nor ought nor anything **but love from thee** but
your love **give recompense** can satisfy it

Thy love is such the love you give to me is so
enormous **I can no way repay** how can I satisfy
you

The heavens reward thee manifold the gods
alone can bless you **I pray** that's what I'm
counting on

Then while we live a long time I hope **in love** I
hope **let's so persevere** let's treat this love very
seriously

That when we live no more it will come   a long
time ahead **we may live ever** people will tell
stories of our love for ever

The connecting thoughts will prepare you to confidently
speak the next phrase of the poem. Also think in terms

of how long the audience might need to digest the words you've given them, so that they are ready for the next bit.

As with the self-written speeches, I tend to leave out the punctuation when I'm writing a text out for myself, and simply leave a space at the end of each phrase. You might feel happy with the text as it is, with punctuation, without spaces. Whatever makes you feel well supported and confident is the right choice for you. And this is a personal 'interpretation'. I want it to inspire you to look at the poem and come up with your own ideas so that you feel you understand it better and could speak it with confidence. You can use the same exercises on your own readings, in order to find a deeper and more satisfying relationship with the text.

 Emma came to see me in an absolute panic. A close friend was getting married and had asked her to read a poem at the wedding. She knew Emma belonged to an amateur drama group and therefore 'knew' she would be the perfect person. She didn't know that Emma had a horror of poetry, had never felt she understood it at school, and whenever the drama group were choosing Shakespeare to perform would pretend to be extra busy at work.

And the poem had been chosen, so there was no room for manoeuvre there! It was to be another wedding favourite, 'If thou must love me', written by Elizabeth Barrett Browning.

> If thou must love me, let it be for nought
> Except for love's sake only. Do not say
> 'I love her for her smile—her look—her way
> Of speaking gently,—for a trick of thought
> That falls in well with mine, and certes brought
> A sense of pleasant ease on such a day'—
> For these things in themselves, Beloved, may
> Be changed, or change for thee,—and love, so wrought,
> May be unwrought so. Neither love me for
> Thine own dear pity's wiping my cheeks dry,—
> A creature might forget to weep, who bore
> Thy comfort long, and lose thy love thereby!
> But love me for love's sake, that evermore
> Thou mayst love on, through love's eternity.

The first thing I got Emma to do was read it out loud – she had read it silently to herself before she arrived and nearly had a nervous breakdown as she felt she barely understood a word of it. She took my advice to read it at a steady pace, and to stop for a moment at the end of each line, and at the other punctuation points in the poem. And immediately some light began to dawn.

My next suggestion to Emma was this: imagine that after the audience have heard you speak each line of the text, they will want to ask a question. You will respond to their question by speaking the next line.

I've written out the questions that Emma and I came up with, and labelled them as 'connecting thoughts', because in performance they will not be spoken. And I also suggested to Emma that she did her own interpretation or paraphrase of each line. The word 'certes' sent us looking for a dictionary, and online Emma quickly found 'certainly' and 'truly' as more contemporary versions of the word. Don't be afraid of using a dictionary, English is an enormous language and there are bound to be loads of words many of us don't know, especially the more old-fashioned ones. This poem is basically a simple heartfelt plea: I love you, and I think you love me, but I want you to love me for the right reasons, because if it's just because of the way I look, or that I amuse you, or that I just happened once or twice to agree with something you said, I could turn out to be a disappointment.

THE TEXT (paraphrased)	CONNECTING THOUGHTS
'If you must love me … let it be for nothing'	nothing but WHAT?
'For nothing but that you love me for my own sake … don't say'	don't say WHAT?
'that you love the way I smile or look … or my way'	your way of WHAT?
'of speaking … don't love me because of the way I think'	HOW do you think?

THE TEXT (paraphrased)	CONNECTING THOUGHTS
'the way I think that sometimes goes along with the way you think … and certainly brought'	brought WHAT?
'a lovely relaxed atmosphere … on one particular day'	WHY can't I love you for these things?
'these things … the things I do, the way I behave, oh Loved One may'	may WHAT?
'well I might change or you might change … and love that has grown'	might WHAT?
'might un-grow … and for goodness sake don't love me because …'	because WHAT?
'because you think I need cheering up and you like cheering me up'	WHY?
'someone who is cheered up might forget to cry … someone who experiences'	WHAT?
'long experience of your cheering up … then I'll lose your love'	so WHAT is the answer?

THE TEXT (paraphrased)	CONNECTING THOUGHTS
'if you love me because you love me … then for ever and ever'	ever and ever WHAT?
'you might stay loving me … and that's real eternal love …'	

RHYTHM EXERCISE 2

It's always good to encourage and renew our feeling for rhythm, especially when dealing with a set text. If we can take our enjoyment of the pulse and music of the text and use that energy when we speak, it will massively add to our confidence. We all know the rhythm of our favourite music has us tapping our toes within seconds. I am ready to confess that I have found myself walking in time to the rhythm of music playing in a department store. Am I alone?

Nursery rhymes usually have strong rhythmic structures:

Hickory, dickory, dock,
The mouse ran up the clock.
The clock struck one,
The mouse ran down,
Hickory, dickory, dock.

Speak the poem out loud, and think of having a little pause at the end of each line. Pause for the time it takes you to move your eye from the end of one line to the beginning of the next. As the last line is the same as the first line you will be aware of a strong sense of beginning and ending, and you'll find that your voice wants to make that clear.

Now, hum the rhythm of the words. What does it sound like?

'MM mm mm MM mm mm MM'
'HICKory DICKory DOCK'

The upper case 'MM's are the heavy beats – this is how rhythm works, in heavier and lighter beats. If you don't emphasize some syllables, everything will sound flat. Try it again, without any emphasis:

'MM MM MM MM MM MM MM'
'HICKORY DICKORY DOCK'

Doesn't sound great, does it?

Humming the rhythm of the text we are going to speak can help us hear and enjoy the ups-and-downs of the piece. Hum the rhythm of a phrase of your choosing, then straight away speak the words. I hope you hear that the words have more life in them, a stronger heartbeat.

READING EXERCISE

I wanted to include something non-poetic, so we're going to look at an extract from *Nicholas Nickleby*, by Charles Dickens. I have made cuts in the section I chose, so that we're not getting bogged down with any characters who haven't been introduced properly. Apologies to Dickens.

The mood of the piece is easy to sum up: joy and excitement about the forthcoming wedding of younger characters in the story.

Now, Tim Linkinwater and Miss La Creevy had met very often, and had always been very chatty and pleasant together—had always been great friends.

'Don't cry!'

'I must,' rejoined Miss La Creevy.

'No, don't,' said Tim. 'Please don't; pray don't.'

'I am so happy!' sobbed the little woman.

'Then laugh,' said Tim. 'Do laugh. Or I'll cry.'

'Why should you cry?' asked Miss La Creevy, smiling.

'Because I'm happy too,' said Tim. 'We are both happy, and I should like to do as you do.

It's a pleasant thing to people like us, who have passed all our lives in the world alone, to see young folks that we are fond of, brought together with so many years of happiness before them.'

'Ah!' cried the little woman with all her heart, 'that it is!'

'Although,' pursued Tim 'although it makes one feel quite solitary and cast away. Now don't it? It's almost enough to make us get married, isn't it?' said Tim.

'Oh, nonsense!' replied Miss La Creevy, laughing. 'We are too old.'

'Not a bit,' said Tim; 'we are too old to be single.

Why shouldn't we both be married, instead of sitting through the long winter evenings by our solitary firesides? Why shouldn't we make one fireside of it, and marry each other?'

'Oh, Mr Linkinwater, you're joking!'

'No, no, I'm not. I'm not indeed,' said Tim. 'I will, if you will. Do, my dear!'

'It would make people laugh so.'

'Let 'em laugh,' cried Tim stoutly; 'we have good tempers I know, and we'll laugh too. Come let's be a comfortable couple.'

Speak the story out loud. Imagine you can see the characters. Look on the internet and find some drawings or paintings from the period. Picture Tim Linkinwater and Miss La Creevy – who although they might think of themselves as 'not young' are perhaps not what we would call 'old'. The atmosphere is warm. Nothing dangerous or horrid is going to happen, just the excitement of a new chapter in their lives.

If you have time, write or type out the text. Put in some spaces between the phrases as we've done before. You don't need to print out the text with the gaps still there if you don't find it useful. But just seeing some space between phrases can help you not to feel rushed.

Now   Tim Linkinwater   and Miss
    La Creevy   had met very often
and had always been very chatty   and pleasant
    together   had always been great friends
'Don't cry!'   [says Tim]

'I must,'   rejoined Miss La Creevy.

'No, don't,'   said Tim

'Please don't   pray don't'

If you really believe in these characters as you tell us about them and speak their words you will help your audience to enjoy the story more. They will see what you see and believe what you believe. And that is the secret of a good reading. Imagine lots of details, and you will easily win over your audience. As usual, you might find it useful to practise with your voice recorder, but when you lack time, space, or opportunity to practise out loud, you can do some very useful work silently.

 As you work on your text, rather than just speaking the words in your head, shape them silently with your mouth. It's good articulation practice. Remind yourself just how long it takes to articulate clearly.

As when you're writing your own speeches, dividing up the text into sections is also useful. You see the shape on the page and are reminded to pause and breathe. You should find it easier to memorize the shape of the story – even if you do not actually memorize the text itself.

I would divide the Dickens text into five sections. The first section is short, and the second section begins 'Don't cry!' The third section begins, 'it's a pleasant thing' and the fourth section begins 'why shouldn't we both be married ...'. The final section is the last two lines. But this is just my own personal preference, you will find your best shape as you read out loud and listen to the characters (and to Charles Dickens) speaking.

PART FOUR
Speeches for all occasions

12. The leaving speech

Whether at work or in your personal life, you may find yourself called upon to do a number of different speeches throughout your life. Whether it is a leaving do, a group meeting, speaking at your local rotary club or anything in between, a focus on role play will be useful here. Just as the queen is expected to wave so you are expected to speak. A reasonable amount of time must be spent with the audience. Extra material must be found, beside a bald 'hello/goodbye/welcome/we shall miss you'. You need to put your own stamp on the role.

For clarity's sake we will focus mostly on speaking in a professional context here, but the theories are just as applicable elsewhere. Here are the most basic areas to think about in this situation, with some possible answers underneath:

What do you want the audience to think about you?
- You are witty/funny

- You are light-hearted

- You are fun to be with

- You are serious at heart

- You are energetic

- You are laid back

What do you want the audience to think about your message?

- (S)he really understands what this occasion is about.

- This message is full of heart.

- It made me remember why I like working for this company.

Is your message ...

- Your opinion, no one else has a say in it?

- The 'party line', which you *have* to deliver?

- The 'party line', which you *want* to deliver?

How do you feel about your message?

- There is only one message (I am good at my job/clever/ the expert/the only one anyone need listen to).

- I have no message, except that I am happy to be here and happy that you are here.

- It's my way of showing how much I value my staff, my team, my job ...

What do you want people to understand, after hearing your message?

- This person really likes us (respects us/values us/thinks we are good company).

- This person understands us better than we thought (s)he did.

- This person is capable of more that we thought (s)he was.

If you can answer all of these questions you'll be getting much closer to successfully pitching whatever speaking it is you have to do. The next thing to look at is the subject matter.

Generating initial material

Like the foundations of a house, it is important to come up with some base material for the construction of a speech. Let's introduce three more questions here:

- What are you comfortable speaking about?

- What would you rather not talk about?

- Are there details about your life that you are happy to confess? (Do you like Mozart but can't bear Beethoven? Do you always wear green socks? Does flying make you nervous?)

We need to be aware here of playing status, and there are personal decisions to be made. I remember reading in a newspaper that some members of the British Royal Family had Tupperware containers full of breakfast cereal on their breakfast table. Whether this is remotely true I have no way of knowing, but perhaps this is not a picture we relish seeing. Perhaps we would rather fill royal breakfast tables with silver plates and imagine uniformed staff serving from fine china. Whether you are addressing your staff or your employers, or have to speak in front of the Queen herself, you need to be aware of your status, of the picture of you that you want to be seen and heard. And with the proliferation of social media and the possibility of every detail of our lives flying around the globe in a split second – should anybody be at all interested – we all need to think about what we might like to see 'in print' after the event.

Fear of revealing all the secrets of our lives needs to be balanced with wanting to best use these occasions so that people feel they know us a bit better, that we have opened up to them a little, even told them the odd secret that 'not a lot of people know'.

TRY IT NOW!

Practise talking into your recorder on any of these subjects:

My favourite piece of music – What is it? Why do you think it is your favourite? How long have you liked it? When did you first hear it? Does it remind you of a particular time or place or person?

My favourite holiday – Where? When? Who with? What did you like?

One thing that I like about myself – That I am prepared to work hard to get what I want; that I have good willpower; that I am a good friend …

One thing I would like to change about myself – I am too self-conscious; I get easily distracted; I am always late …

Something I believe in passionately – Saving the environment; providing for my family; the importance of voting …

The topics can be anything you like, but here are a few more ideas to focus on if you're struggling:

• One thing about myself that I laugh about

• One thing I'm proud of

• One thing I'd very much like to learn from others

 Don't go into subservient mode: 'I am so sorry to interrupt you when you're obviously having such a good time … and I won't take up to much of your time … I just wanted to say a few words about …'. Well, you are interrupting. And you are being very boring, worrying about being boring. I'm never a fan of, 'and I'd just like to say,' or 'first I'd like to say'. Are we then going to get, 'and second I'd like to say' and 'third I'd like to say'? If you have something to say, say it.

CASE STUDY

Marco is the Managing Director of an international company. He did not feel at his most confident doing the 'Hello' or 'Goodbye' speeches that were so often part of his job. Not that he didn't care about visiting CEOs or employee's birthdays, he just didn't know how to make it into a speech that he could relax with and enjoy. This is how we went about trying to de-stress one of these situations.

First there were questions we decided he needed to answer. What was the centre of the speech, the main reason Marco needed to speak? Someone quite high up in the company was leaving to get married, so there was going to be a big party. What were Marco's main concerns? He didn't want to put a downer on the whole proceedings: 'Oh this is so sad', 'Let's all cry into our drinks', etc. But he also didn't want to just get up and say, 'Oh we all know that Maria is leaving. All the best Maria', and then have someone hand her a leaving gift. The occasion needed a bit of care and respect.

We worked together to write the speech, my job being simply to make suggestions. Sometimes the game I play with actors is to say, 'Oh you don't really need to say that line, do you? Let's cut it', and then wait for them to blow up and tell me I must be stupid and isn't that the most important line their character speaks? At which point I say: 'That's fine, you can keep the line, now I know how much you want it. How passionately you feel about it.' That's the way Marco and I worked – whether the line was my suggestion or his, if it didn't feel good to Marco when he spoke it, out it went, and we thought of something else. He needed to feel that this was exactly what he wanted to say or he would not stand any chance of being a confident speaker.

Here's the opening of Marco's speech:

It has been a very busy week
Our ginger tomcat had kittens
We're looking for a good home for them   if you
     might be interested
and there's a new *Doctor Who* on TV   too much
     excitement

You could win 12 million pounds in the Lottery this
     weekend
so I really had better not keep you too long tonight
in case you still need to buy your ticket

and with Valentine's Day fast approaching
ebay are offering 200 mini chocolate hearts for
     £2.20
an absolute bargain   where true love is
     concerned

Now this is all nonsense, all flim-flam. But I wanted Marco to think about subtext. The word 'subtext' can help us focus on the underlying message, what lies behind the words.

We need to understand that very often the subtext is more important than the 'text': the subtext is the message that the audience will really receive.

So what did Marco really want his message to be at Maria's leaving party? I advised him to think about this subtext very carefully, and this was his conclusion:

'Hi, aren't we having a good time? And isn't the company generous to put on this spread? And isn't Maria going to look back on this evening with pleasure? And aren't I a great boss, here partying with you all? And of course we really are sorry to lose Maria.'

Phrasing the subtext as a question or series of questions can give your speech a strong and outgoing energy.

That's what Marco wanted people to remember. And now his job was to find some words to clothe the message, some words that he would feel comfortable saying. Marco loves his Italian home, in the beautiful Tuscan countryside near to Siena, and any thought of weddings made him think of home and family, so he decided to use the Valentine's Day theme, and include a little story:

In Italy   we have little chocolate and hazelnut treats.
Which we call   Baci   'kisses'

They are a popular Valentine's Day gift in Italy

Each chocolate Baci   is wrapped in   a message
    of affection   love   or friendship

The notes   have quotes   from the world's
    best-known poets
The quotes are translated into different languages
They are very educational

Maria   is about to be married   on   Valentine's
    Day
we are sad to lose her
we have included among her presents   a box of
    Baci chocolates

She will give them to those she loves
but we hope she will save at least one for herself

I will allow myself   one small *baci*   of the
    non-chocolate kind   on the cheek

Maria   we wish you every good wish   for your
    new life
A new home   a new country

I would like to propose a toast   so please raise
    your glasses   to Maria

If the words you are speaking seem to be giving one message and the tone of your voice or your demeanour gives another, which message are people going to believe? The sound of your voice or the way you behave? Always make sure to match the two elements.

Talking about something that affects everyone is a good starting point. The weather is not to be sniffed at. Very British perhaps, but at least we can laugh at ourselves. 'Three days of a heat wave and we can't wait for it to snow.' 'Five wet and windy days in a row and I'm tired of my umbrella blowing inside out.' The audience might think, 'Oh, how true,' or 'That pink tie he's wearing really does go with the blue suit, who would have thought it?' or 'How long is this going to go on? I want to get back to the bar.' But it really doesn't matter. It's a party. It's not 'serious'.

Then we can add something a bit more personal. Remember that you always make the choice as to what you want to reveal. You might feel more comfortable with a more 'vanilla' style of text, so below I've written out a simpler version of the speech for Maria's party. Delivered with focus and heart it would work perfectly well.

Good evening   everyone
Thank you all   so much   for being here tonight
It's a sad time and a happy time

Sad because Maria is leaving us   happy that
    Maria has named her wedding day

Such a beautiful name   Maria   very Italian
And being Italian   some of you might think I will
    now begin to sing
But I promise you   that would not be such a
    good idea   I am a disgrace to my country

Maria   you have played such an important role in
    this company   and we shall miss you
But we are thrilled   for you   about the new life
    ahead
And Valentine's Day is such a clever day   to
    choose for your wedding.

Please accept these gifts   from all of us
They come with all our best wishes.
We hope it will be   *arrivederci*   that we shall
    see you again

I would like to propose a toast   so please raise
    your glasses   to Maria

If you're feeling inspired, never allow yourself
to go into an, 'Oh, I just need to think about it
first; I'll write it tomorrow' sort of mood. No
you won't. Think with your fingers or with your mouth.

Public speaking needs practice like any other performance activity. If you were a pianist you'd need to practise your scales. Only then do you get to play in front of an audience. And just because a professional performer looks cool, it doesn't mean that they're not nervous: the moment before they step out in front of the audience might feel terrifying. So when you feel nerves you are not alone. You don't know, and you will not know how it will go until it is 'going'.

It might seem surprising, but many clients find a great deal of relief when they accept the 'role' of performer. You are not in your own front room talking to friends and family. The event needs planning. You need strategy. You need to practise.

13. The interview

One of the most terrifying bits of confident speaking most people encounter is the job interview. Many of us find it really difficult talking about ourselves, and feel like we're being boastful by talking about our own talents and experience. So one technique that can be helpful here is to think about ourselves in the third person. We are often clearer and more positive about others than about ourselves.

 Try practising out loud, speaking into your recorder. What are the special qualities, abilities, talents, skills of this person (you)? Rather than saying 'I' use the third person 'he' or 'she'. You could have a rehearsal if you like, talking about a good friend. Why is it that you like this person? Why do you value them as a friend? Are there stories you could tell where we see their friendship in action?

At every possible opportunity, be active. Speak out loud. Having a recorder in your hand will guide your speaking, and help you learn to listen to yourself. Alternatively, you could write down any ideas you have as you prepare for an interview. That would be better than just having random, rambling thoughts. But this book is called confident speaking, so we need you to be vocal.

Exercises to help you prepare

As you sit and wait to be called in to the interview room, or as you sit waiting for the first question, your head will be full of instructions and reminders. So you need to practise, at times when life is less demanding, being 'in the moment'. What does that mean? Simply seeing what is in front of you. Simply hearing the sounds in the room. Simply being aware that you are breathing. In, out, in, out. So that when the more demanding event is happening, you will be fully alive to that moment, and listening to what is being said to you, rather than caught up in thoughts of yesterday or tomorrow. The chattering mind easily blocks out what is actually going on in that live moment.

FOCUS EXERCISE 1

I refer to this exercise as 'Watching Your Breath'. Simply being alive means that breath moves in and out of your body – you do not have to 'try' to breathe as you are already doing it. Just be aware of which part of the cycle you are in: observe the breath going out and then some new breath coming in. Observe it almost as if it were happening to someone else. You might find it useful to silently repeat, 'the breath is going out, the breath is going out …' followed by 'the breath is coming in …', to firmly focus yourself on what is happening. This is a kind of meditation, and the words act as a mantra. You should find it relaxing, but it may take some practice. Your chattering mind will want to ambush you and try to persuade you to be busy thinking and making lots of decisions. For just one minute, watch your breath.

FOCUS EXERCISE 2
Look out of the window into the garden. Imagine someone needs you to describe to them the picture you see. A bus goes by, or a bird or a plane. How detailed could you make your picture? Is there something that attracts your attention? A colour, a beautiful person, the sun shining? Be aware of the chair you sit on: feel your seat against its seat, enjoy the support it gives. Are you breathing? Count the books on a bookshelf. Can you hear music? How would you describe it? We all miss so much, because we are busy chattering. Bring yourself into the present. You don't want to let your interview pass you by, do you? Practise this for just one minute.

What do you want from the job?
You might think that the point of an interview is to prove to the interviewers that you're the right person for the job. This is true, but you also need to be as clear as possible about what *you* are looking for in a role.

THINK ABOUT IT

We need to look at the whole situation from as many angles as possible. In all of these confident speaking situations you are not alone. You do not have to 'play the scene' solo. Parts of the event may be monologue, but not all. And as every actor knows, we need to recognize the difference between a monologue and a soliloquy. A soliloquy would mean that you are the only person in the room as you speak. But with public speaking you are not alone. You may just happen to have all the words for a time, but that doesn't mean that there's no one else in the scene.

Acting techniques teach us to question what our character wants. When we've decided what we want, we need to decide what we are prepared to do to get it.

We need to open ourselves up to the 'other' – in this case the people who have a job to offer. We were interested enough to apply for the job, and they are interested enough to give us an interview. We need to find what other common ground we have.

RECORDING EXERCISE 1

Speak freely into your recorder. Why do you want this job? Is it just because it is a job and at the moment you don't have one? Is it a better job? Better in that there is more money? Better in terms of status? Do you want the job at any cost, in the sense that it means getting up at 5am every morning and you would need to work some weekends, and you'd have to cope with them not offering a free gym membership? Honesty is your best starting position.

What does the job want from you?

Take the time and trouble on this one. Research the company offering the interview. Use the internet; there is a lot of information we can freely access. What does the company do? Is there anything you might not like about them? Anything you might find disagreeable? What job are they offering? Ask the company themselves, or the recruiters, for as much information as possible.

RECORDING EXERCISE 2

Talk all of your findings into your recorder. How do you like the sound of what you are hearing about the company? What are the questions you want to ask in your interview?

 Take time to think about how you will behave when you get into the interview. When we get into speaking mode – and especially monologue mode – we tend to turn off or at least turn down some of the listening mode. We prepare our little speech, and we are going to say it. Because that's what we have come for, isn't it? But it's important to remember that an interview is still a conversation – you can say all the right things and still leave the interviewer with the abiding memory that you talked too much.

RECORDING EXERCISE 3

Keep speaking into your recorder. You now have some information about the job. How well would it suit you? Would it use all of your skills? Is there anything particular about the job that you would relish, a chance to focus on some aspect of your career that has been on the back burner? Are there any particular aspects of the job that you would need to brush up on? Does it match where you want to be in two years? In five? In ten?

Always attempt to turn any part of your discovery – about who you are, what you want, what you aim to be doing with your life – into a positive. A company may want someone who is skilled in some areas but willing to be trained-up in others.

You might need to accept a lower status for a time, and be a new boy or girl at the beginning. Would you see this as a great opportunity or an insult to the list of experience already on your CV?

What have you got to offer them? What do they have to offer you? What are your best qualities; what are your worst qualities? Why might you choose this company over another? Why might the company choose you over someone else?

RECORDING EXERCISE 4

Imagine yourself as the boss of the company you are interviewing for. If you were the boss, what would you look for in a candidate? How might you go about finding the right person for the job, if you were them? What might you ask them? Come up with at least five questions. Turn off the recorder and write down the questions the boss would want to ask. Turn your recorder back on, refocus as the candidate for the job and ask yourself the questions. How good are your answers? If you were the boss, would you give you the job?

Your response to any question in an interview should last no more than two minutes maximum. If they want any more, any details, they can ask for it.

Pitching yourself

We all spend a lot of time and energy putting together a CV that we hope will precisely and concisely give all the facts any employer might need to know. So when we get asked to improvise a verbal overview of all this information panic can quickly set in. We might see a copy of the CV there in front of the interviewer. 'Why don't they read it?' we think. 'Why do they want me to tell them when they could read a perfectly-phrased version?' Because they have already read it. That's why they invited you in for an interview.

Now they have you sitting in front of them, they want a real, live, transaction. They want to meet you. Hear your voice. Get to know you a bit. And work out whether they want to spend 35-plus hours a week with you for the foreseeable future.

RECORDING EXERCISE 5
Read out some of your CV and aim to convert the written style that you've used into something more conversational. If there were three things you were most proud of in your life what would they be? If there were three things that you most wanted to achieve in your next job what would they be? If there were three things about you that you most wanted an employer to know what would they be?

One question I was regularly asked by director friends as they compiled interview lists for the production of a play was: 'Are they a good company member?' Not: 'Are they a good actor?' They knew I wouldn't suggest anyone I didn't think could act, but they wanted to make sure they would work well within a company. I know you are probably not interviewing as an actor, but companies are still looking for good group members.

'How do you like to work?' is a question you could be asked. Do you prefer to be usually within group situations? Or do you prefer to be given a task and allowed to go off and find you own best way of dealing with it?

There are lots more permutations to all of these questions. The internet is full of questions that might be asked together with examples of answers you could or should give. Take from them, learn from them. But don't forget that living a lie is for most people not very comfortable. You might answer the question 'correctly', but having talked the talk you then will have to walk the walk.

What is the worst question they can ask?

It's tempting to ignore this, and hope that it never happens. But given the number of clients who tell me how they suffer through whole meetings, waiting for the question they don't want to answer, isn't it better to find a solution in advance? It might not be the perfect answer, the one the questioner wants to hear. It might include an apology: 'I'm sorry, I don't have that information right now.' But it shows that you've thought about it and that you want to engage with the questioner. That should count for something.

REMEMBER THIS!!! It's very important to make sure you answer the question that is asked, not the one you hoped they would ask, and had prepared an answer for. I think we all imagine whole conversations, especially for events we are keen to make a success. We think: 'They'll say this and I'll answer that. Then they'll ask this, and I can tell them that.' And then they don't, and we have the answer to the un-asked question there, already in our mouths. It's hard, but put a stop on it. Dare to be silent for a moment while you digest what they actually did ask. You don't have to give the whole answer in one breath. You could play for time. Give part of the answer. See how that is received. Even ask the interviewer if they need more detail, if you're unsure. This is dialogue, not a monologue.

Be an individual

A radio programme I was listening to the other day voiced the belief that employers nowadays are getting bored with the 'stock' answers that interviewees are prone to trot-out. We've all spent too much time on the internet. We've learned the content of 'if they ask this question, this is the answer you should give …' websites. The question they suggested on the programme as an example of the new, wily interview strategies that employers are now starting to use went something like this. 'If you were shrunk to the size of a pencil and put inside a blender, how would you get out?' I really had to rack my brain on this one. Just because I am the *size* of a pencil doesn't mean that I *am* a pencil. And how big is a pencil? Presuming that the blender is not turned on, I would use my nails to climb up the sides of the blender and make myself as narrow as possible to squeeze out of the central hole in the lid. If the blender was turned on I would jump up (very quickly!) using the energy of the blades – the wind they create as they move – to lift me towards the top of the blender and towards the hole in the lid. You might think my answer is very silly, and you might be right. And you might just think that it's a silly question. But if it is asked, it's better that you come up with some kind of answer – it's not about being right, it's about showing your personality and unique thinking.

Selling yourself

The job that you are interviewing for could, on the face of it, have little to do with being a salesman, but we are all selling something. We all have to believe, and show, that we have something to offer. Something that we find valuable. Something that we believe others could find useful. You might even be asked to do some kind of sales pitch at an interview. Let's practise.

RECORDING EXERCISE 6

Think of something you find useful. It might be something very simple, but that saves you energy, or saves you time. How might you 'sell' it to someone else? I like making soup, for example, but the really boring bit is blending the vegetables so that it looks like soup rather than just well-cooked vegetables. I used to have to transfer it into a rather ancient food processor we happened to have, which did the job in about 30 seconds. Then the food processor needed taking apart and washing, and that seemed to take for ever. And then I discovered one little gadget that changed my soup-making life. I plug it in and stick its little moving blades in the saucepan I've cooked the soup in. Thirty or forty seconds of activity. Job done. Tiny amount of washing up. Happy man.

It could be a website that solves problems for you, or an App. The kind of pasta that reminds you of Italian holidays. The kind of razor that gives you the best shave. The kind of exercise system that makes you feel fit but doesn't take too much of your time. Focus on how you might promote whatever it is to someone else. In 'selling' the idea or product, you are 'selling' yourself, as someone who values something and has enthusiasm.

Like every story it can be told in different ways. There will be shorter and longer versions of the story. Examine and practise every version you can think of. Would the story be told differently to a group of women than a group of men? Might the relative age of your audience make a difference?

THINK ABOUT IT

Phone a friend

If you have friends who have similar interests, who are also planning for events like presentations or interviews, you could be useful to each other. Be a sounding board. Give support and encouragement. Always be very specific with each other, as to exactly what the task is. If you decided on a length of time for whatever you are delivering, did you stick to time? Did you sound rushed? Was your articulation clear? If you have the chance to work in a larger space, take it.

Imagine you have a larger audience. You will need to take time to breathe. If your voice needs to travel further you'll need more energy. Get used to speaking up and out. An interview is always a conversation, so why not get some rehearsal in beforehand?

---

14. Meetings and conversations

Whether the event you need to take part in relates to your present employment, or an interview for a new job, some of the preparation will be very much the same.

Whatever the specifics of the situation, each event will have a purpose, and the clearer you are about that purpose and your role in the proceedings, the stronger your performance will be.

 Either write some notes or if possible speak into your voice recorder answering the following questions:

- *Why* is the meeting happening?

- *Why* do you need to be there?

- Do you have an overall *objective* for being at the meeting? (i.e. to be a spokesperson for your company, or to speak better than you ever have before, or to be offered a job).

- Have you *prepared* all the material you will need to use in the meeting? Have you armed yourself with answers to difficult questions?

- What is your *status* relative to the other participants? Are there people you want to impress? Is there someone you would like to forge a closer working relationship with?

- What would be the *best outcome* for you?

When you enter the space you need to send out strong confident energy to anyone already there. Sitting or standing, breathe out your strong energy. Let it fill the room. Imagine that you can see the energy travelling to every corner. Remember, if you are feeling apprehensive and nervous your breathing will tend to tighten and then your voice will sound weaker. It could even look and sound as if you don't really want to be there. So take plenty of time when you breathe in and recognize that breathing out is a kind of affirmation: it will signal that you are committed to fully entering the situation. It can be useful – especially if you're in a situation where you expect emotions to run high – to imagine the event as a scene from a play or film. You play a part in the scene. You are a character. You function within that situation. This will help you to remain objective.

How you are feeling and what you are thinking at this particular moment – important as both are to us all – might be irrelevant. There is a job to be done, a situation to be resolved, an action to fulfil, an objective to achieve. If you suspect that someone is likely to speak against you or over you, forewarned can be forearmed. If you are prepared before the event you will be better able to strengthen yourself. Of course you don't know for certain what's going to happen, but if you keep breathing deeply you'll be ready for each unexpected turn.

Making eye contact

It's important that we meet the eyes of the people we are talking to (but not to stare at them!). It can sometimes be difficult to look at other people if we know they are looking at us, so perhaps we need to think in terms of sharing the looks. Your turn, my turn, so to speak. With a few shared looks in the middle!

It can be a habit to look away as we respond to someone. There are two points of interest here. Firstly, if we look away all the time when we are speaking, we might miss how a partner reacts. We could miss some information that might help us know what to do next. It's a bit like throwing a ball and not knowing where it lands, or not seeing if someone catches it. If you don't realize that your partner now has the ball you might try to throw them another ball when they're not ready for it.

Secondly, when we look away as we speak, it could indicate that we've gone into reflective mode, thinking about things, rather than focussing. When we are having a conversation it's better to think *of* something rather than about it. I will say to clients: 'When we are here together I will think *of* you, because I can do that in an active way. Before you arrive and after you leave, I can think *about* you.' I can reflect, in private, with no responsibility to communicate with others.

This is just one way of describing it; you might prefer an alternative. The important thing is that if you are reflective it will be difficult to engage with others. The kind of energy we use to reflect is quite different to that with which we are active and communal. You need to be interested in what the 'other' is doing, and how you can communicate with them. You won't always get a clear 'view' of course. Some people are masters at either hiding their feelings or putting on a poker face. But to be alive and active in the space, with the other people in the space, is your best bet to achieve some kind of togetherness.

Making friends with others

We can call a meeting a transaction. You do something, so what does the other person do? If you act as if you want to engage – to have a conversation – but continue to monologue, your partner might get confused. If you do feel yourself going into a pre-planned answer and want to remind yourself of the question actually asked try this: repeat to yourself, silently, the last three or four words of your conversation partner's question. Sometimes you could even speak the words out loud, but I wouldn't advise you to do that more than once or twice. '… did I enjoy the work? I did enjoy the work, but I didn't feel I was being stretched …'

 It is all too easy to get too caught up in ourselves, our own thoughts, our own feelings.

When that happens not only is there little eye contact, perhaps we do not really see or hear the other person at all. It all stems from anxiety of course, the pressure of delivering a message and engaging with an audience.

 Practise this in relaxed moments. Notice what someone is wearing and what they look like, and imagine you want to write a story about them. How might you describe them? What do you see? After the event you could write down some of what you noticed.

Try it in public spaces – a bus, a train. Find some words that describe your experience. Don't worry if you are not producing a literary masterpiece; just be as clear as you can.

Engaging with others

Recall a conversation you recently had. It could be useful to write down what you remember, or record it. What was it about? Who spoke the most? What do you remember most? Can you think of things you wanted to say but didn't get the chance to? Either the time ran out, or one of you had to leave. Or the other person was, as you remember it, hogging the conversation a bit. If it was a face-to-face meeting, what were you wearing? What was the other person wearing? How would you describe the style of clothes they were wearing if you wanted someone else to understand as clearly as possible?

You might find that you remember the atmosphere of the conversation better than the particulars of subject, dialogue, or dress. If you find yourself remembering in terms of, 'I felt he didn't give me time to say what I thought,' or 'I felt she was rather dismissive when I mentioned something that mattered a lot to me', stop for a moment and wonder – could there have been similar moments for your conversation partner? Did you give time to listen to their point of view? Did you give them time to really finish their story?

We could watch and listen to someone in conversation with us and imagine the speed and rhythm and energy they use as a kind of dance. How does your 'dance' compare with the way your conversation partner is 'dancing'? Are you slower or faster than them? Smoother, or more syncopated? Louder or quieter?

If you are doing a waltz and they are doing rock and roll, what are your choices? Would you like to rock and roll? You might have a better chance of achieving your aims and objectives if you both do the same dance. If you feel strongly that nothing can be gained by rocking and rolling, then you have to persuade them to waltz, by staying with the speed and rhythm and energy that you have chosen to communicate your message with.

Alternatively, you might view your conversation partner's energy – the speed at which they speak, the volume they use, the 'music' of their voice – as a particular colour. If they offer you a hot colour like red or orange and you respond to them with a cooler colour like blue or green your response might seem inappropriate. We are very affected by the tone and energy of someone's voice. We often take more notice of that tone than the actual words spoken. So if the colours don't match, the response could sound like lack of interest in or lack of empathy with your conversation partner.

Notice your partner's breathing patterns. Are they slow or fast? Are you aware of the upper part of their body moving more than the middle part? If you control your breathing you can encourage them to breathe more deeply. If you are both grounded it should be easier to have a rational and productive conversation.

Practise in more relaxed situations first, without staring! By copying someone else's breathing pattern for a few minutes you may get some idea of how they feel, which can be useful in a business situation. And focussing outside of ourselves will always be useful. Once you've tuned in to your partner's breathing patterns you can make a more fruitful decision as to how you can best respond. Does breathing the way they breathe make you feel better or worse? You have a choice.

KEY TERM

Most people would think it is not a healthy option to breathe very quickly for any length of time. When we **hyperventilate** the chemical balance in the body changes. The term means what it says; our 'ventilating' or breathing is 'hyper', or too much. We take in too much air and consequently we usually feel less in control of our feelings, less stable, and less able to make rational decisions. We link this state with anxiety, nervousness.

If someone is breathing quickly you don't want to base the atmosphere of your interaction around that, so try to ground them using one of two techniques:

1. Use the kind of smooth, controlled, vocal patterns you want them to use; they should pick up on this from you.

2. If the first technique doesn't work, for no longer than ten seconds do exactly what they are doing: the same rhythmic patterns/speed/volume/intonation patterns. Then revert to your own smooth and steady speech pattern. You may need to repeat this two or three times.

You are playing the hero with option two, fearlessly going into this hyper state to bring your partner back to safety. But if you can calm them down your conversation will be less fraught, so everybody benefits.

Small talk can be big talk

We could start with something simple. If I were asked, 'do you like football?' it wouldn't be honest to answer anything but 'no'. But the conversation doesn't have to end there, when it has hardly begun. I could make an offer: 'You *do* like football?' The person then could tell me about their interest in the game. And yes, I know this could prove interminable, but what we can refer to as 'small talk' involves important human interaction. Most of us need it, and I want to show that I am willing to take part in this conversation game.

I could move to another sport. Although I am no sportsman and never have been, I could dredge up an old story about when I was duty-bound to 'enter the field' of cricket. I won't tell you why I was duty-bound right now, because that really would be boring, and I was such a disaster that I was soon asked to leave the field. Though I did tell them right at the beginning that I couldn't bowl straight.

This game is called 'Do Not Block Your Partner', and consists of keeping conversation going using conjunctions to answer mundane questions in a more interesting way.

The word 'no' can be used. But consider what might happen if you added the word 'but' or 'and'. For example: 'Have you ever been to Majorca?' 'No, **but** we did have a holiday on the Spanish mainland.' 'Have you ever had a camping holiday?' 'No, **and** I'll tell you why – my youngest

173

has asthma. She loves sleeping outside. But her asthma gets worse.' If the conversation seems to grind to a halt there are lots of moves possible.

Think in terms of keeping the game going for longer, rather than winning or losing. Sometimes you might – to use a sports image – need to do a bit of nifty footwork if someone else is hogging the ball too much or you feel you've suffered quite enough of their story about the worst hotel in the world in wherever. Make a bold move. You've got holidays, Spain and Majorca, camping, children, and illness as possible subjects already, and there are thousands more to choose from. Take your pick and make a move.

Major companies send employees on courses where they are advised on small talk. Small talk can be big business. So get practising.

Can you hear my voice at the back?

Each of us will have patterns of behaviour that feel comfortable – and this particularly applies to the volume at which we speak. We don't want to go above that comfort level or it would feel like shouting. And that we do not want to do. But quite often our sense of what is right and appropriate gets a bit skewed, and many clients have complained that they receive comments about their volume levels. So we do exercises to help them find more vocal strength, and I hasten to reassure them that the voice they're producing sounds nothing like shouting. But it can still take time to acclimatize to the extra power they are producing.

Formal conversations

There are lots of examples of more formal conversations – where you're still essentially chatting with someone, but the constraints are stricter and there is more pressure. The most obvious example I can think of is a TV or radio interview. I am sometimes asked to take part in radio programmes. The call usually comes in at the last moment – when some piece of news that might need a 'voice expert' comment has surfaced. Most will have no idea who I am. I'm not being modest, it's just the truth of the situation. So in most senses I am not on the radio as 'Alan'. They are not interested in 'Alan', they just want an 'expert' comment.

Sometimes it's done on the phone, sometimes in a studio. I know very well that all in all it isn't very important, as news items go, and if a really hot story breaks I'll be cut out. Does that make me feel good, or bad? Well, I know the situation. There's usually no payment for my efforts, but I like having a bit of a chat, and the actor in me likes a bit of 'performance'.

So how do I work out my 'expert performance'? What do I want to say? What do I need to say? There'll be no script, and it could last all of 45 seconds. A recent programme I was on focussed on some comments made by the head of a TV station: his view was that actors should be told not to mumble in TV dramas. What is the expert view? If actors are going to be asked or told not to mumble who's going to ask or tell them? The boss himself? Does the expert think the boss is right?

My first decisions related to the difference between the 'expert' opinion and my opinion. I, Alan, might want to say: 'What a load of rubbish. What do you know about actors and acting, Mr Bossman?' But the expert might need to say: 'He's got a point … I'm sure some people would agree with him … especially with the statistics – although younger people tend to make the TV programmes, older people are more likely to be the viewers … and perhaps what needs to be considered is the amount of background music … And of course contemporary speaking styles might seem less 'formal' and perhaps less clearly articulated …' Different people will have different views and it is my job as a coach/teacher/expert to see the situation from as many points of view as possible.

 The presenter or interviewer is not your friend. They are not there to help you relax, they just want to make good TV and radio programmes. If you keep repeating the presenter's name, it only serves to weaken your position, in my opinion. It can so easily sound like pleading – I hear a subtext of 'please listen to me', 'you're not letting me finish my point or you would see that I am right', 'I'm going to say it all again as you obviously don't understand yet …' The actual words could be something like, 'But David … If you would let me finish, David … But the Prime Minister has been very clear on this, David …'. It doesn't sound like confident speaking.

If the subject is a debate, and the interviewer feels that you are ill-prepared they might want to unnerve you. Do not confuse your function with their function.

Lauren was very experienced and comfortable doing presentations, but now needed to be a spokesperson for her company on TV. 'The presenter and I were talking away beforehand,' she said, 'having a good discussion about the questions she would ask and the kind of answers I would give, and how much time we would have on air. Then it was time for the actual programme. It was like the whole scene turned into technicolour. The energy was suddenly very different – a performance energy, I suppose we could call it. And it really shocked me at first.'

Whatever situation you are required to speak in, performance energy can be quite scary at first. Actors get used to it, in the very practical sense that even if you are doing an intimate scene for two characters, which in real life no one else would be expected to overhear, the audience will not be appreciative if they feel left out and in need of a hearing aid. It is not only a question of volume, but of reaching out and making contact with an audience.

It can be tempting to believe that just because the microphone is close to your mouth and the camera is right in front of your face you only need to give a small performance. These are the exercises I taught Lauren:

1. See your whole energy – both your vocal energy and your inner desire to engage with an audience – as not stopping at the microphone or camera, but going through to the outside world. It can be useful to imagine just one special person out there who desperately wants you to communicate with them.

2. Warm up your voice by humming. This is a great way to make you sound strong and give you a good presence. I taught Lauren the humming exercises shown in chapter one.

Then, when in the TV studio, I advised Lauren to imagine an energy channel linking her with the presenter. You can even imagine that every bit of energy you give out – whether it's a soft sound or a loud sound, or just a facial or hand gesture – is so full of life that it bounces off any surface it meets, and the energy actually continues to grow rather than dying away. As Lauren said afterwards: 'Now I know that's what I have to do. When the camera or mike is on, go into performance gear.'

Conclusion

Communication is hard, and we all know that from time to time words slip out that neither express our true intention nor show us in a particularly good light. We'd love to rewind and play that scene all over again, now we've had what feels like a trial run, but often as not we can't.

In this book we've looked at everything from basic breathing and vocal training to planning and preparing for specific events. I have focussed in on as many types of occasion where you need confident speaking as possible, and I hope you feel empowered to go out and speak wherever you need to. Confident speaking is always a work in progress, though, and you may feel you'd like further advice on how to improve your vocal communication skills. Even the most seasoned performers stumble every once in a while, and though nothing beats simply practising your speaking, here are some quick thoughts that might iron out the odd sticky moment and help you move forward on your quest for confident speech. Then, you can look at the Speaker's Toolkit I've compiled at the back of the book, which has more exercises and ideas for you.

- The sounds of the English language are made as we breathe out. The breathing muscles tend to get locked up when we are thinking, listening, and waiting. Remind yourself that you are clever enough to multi-task and breathe well whatever else you might be doing.

- Unless we breathe deeply it will be difficult to stay calm and keep the words we speak under control.

- Just because the person asking you a question speaks quickly doesn't mean you have to answer quickly. Neither does it necessarily mean that they are trying to put you on the spot, it could be just their speaking style.

- There are different ways to tell the same story, depending on your take on the event. See the story from a different angle and you might find exciting new ideas to engage your audience with.

- Imagine yourself as a musical instrument – your speaking partner might be a trumpet when you're a violin. Both instruments can play beautifully and make an important contribution to the music being played. But they need find a way to play together in a manner that is still truthful to their nature.

- Think of yourself as a vehicle with gears, and the content of your speech as being either on the flat or going uphill or going downhill. Imagine the gear that you would need to be in to drive smoothly. It could be boring if the landscape was totally flat for the whole journey. Think of rising to a climax, gliding down after you have hit the heights, and allowing yourself to coast again until you hit another major point.

- If someone asks an important question it can take time to find the best answer. You might feel that you are a 'slow thinker', but you could decide to take your audience with you, in instalments, rather than getting nervous in too long a silence. First, respond in the simplest way to the question. Your subtext will be, 'I hear you, but I want to do justice to you and to myself and to the question.' You might say: 'That's interesting, and I can tell you straight away that I totally agree with the first part of your question; I need a moment to think about the second part.' As you speak you will already be sorting out what you want to say in your full and final statement.

- When you feel tempted to react to a comment as if it were some personal slight, pause and silently count to five. Could there be another interpretation of what was said? Could you have misunderstood the other person's sense of humour? Might it be wise to take time to consider all your options?

If we believe newspaper reports, employers regularly complain that 'soft skills' are not being given enough time and attention in schools, and one of those skills is simply the ability to verbally communicate fluently. The number of hours we all spend in lone communication with computers and other mechanical devices doesn't help – this is one of the reasons I've focussed so much in this book on speaking out loud and audio recording. We can still get nervous trying to find the right words even when we're alone with our voice recorder! When stress levels rise we feel like we've been put on the spot, so I've included the comments about actors in the book not to encourage you to change careers, but to give you faith. These are the professionals, and they know very well that finding the right word in the right moment takes great skill and focus and will always to a degree be in the lap of the gods. They would also tell us that this is part of the fun and the excitement! I'd presume a sports player would say the same thing. If you really know who will win the game what's the point in playing?

I've also laid great stress on the importance of believing that you have, inside, a unique personality and set of abilities. If you don't play the game how will you find out if you could win? And if you do lose one game does it mean you will lose the match? You may just have to learn to play better, or plan your game in a different way. And losing one type of game might just be a hint that there's another better game waiting for you round the corner. It could be scary, but also full of excitement and opportunities.

We've found in this book that there are two major areas we need to focus on and plan for regarding our confident speaking events. First, we need to decide exactly what this event is, what our part in the event is and what it is all in aid of. And then we need to recognize that as well as being something that needs thought, writing and an emotional connection, we also need to prepare physically. An instrument is needed to physically deliver the goods, and our body is that instrument.

I totally believe there is neither a perfect way to speak nor any perfect form of the English language that everyone should use. But just as if we wanted to run a marathon or climb a mountain, we need to get fit. Most of us are busy and the thought that yet more activities need cramming in will not be welcome, but you can exercise your vocal muscles in lots of different ways from singing in the bath to reading bedtime stories to children. And children can be very useful: if the dragon or monster doesn't sound scary or the princess doesn't sound beautiful you will be told. We all get used to speaking in a rather limited way, to the point where we get nervous of trying alternative vocal sounds. Reading a story offers you a chance to practise a bit of acting. So get reading. You might even enjoy it!

Other voice practice opportunities are detailed in the Speaker's Toolkit. You can go through these exercises once you've finished the book, and go back to them at any point when you feel your speaking needs a bit of brushing up.

What else do I hope you've learned from the contents of the book?

We all know the old saying: 'If you don't ask the right question, don't be surprised if you don't get the right answer.' Rehearsal will offer you some wonderful tools, not least of which will be the chance to discover what it is you really want to say. This busy world increasingly demands that we get to the point as quickly as possible, otherwise we waste not only other people's time but their precious energy, not to mention our own resources.

I also hope you've come away with the idea that confident speaking is as much about the audience as it is the speaker. It has often been said that you know you've done a good job teaching when you yourself feel you've learned something. Even if it's not true across the board, I think it begs some interesting questions. You might have planned on using five points to take your audience from beginning to end of your message. But if you can find a way to check in with them they might be able to tell you that two plus two makes four without you needing to tell them. This could benefit both parties – they'll feel clever for knowing something before they've been told, and you'll save time and energy because you don't need to tell a story they already know. And it will strengthen your relationship with them. They'll listen better because they'll want to see if they can jump ahead again.

PowerPoint is still overused or simply not used in a way that serves either speaker or listeners. Be clear why you need a picture or diagram; include in your rehearsal time a verbal description of exactly how you want your audience to view the screen, right to left or top to bottom; and tell yourself exactly what you want people to see. Only have the bare minimum of words on each screen: you are the one telling the story, not the machine.

Unless a presentation or speech was less than two or three minutes in length I don't see, in general, the benefit of speaking without a script. People often get unnecessarily hung up on speaking 'by heart', and make themselves even more nervous in the process. You do need to practise with the script though, in order to use it well. But if it's not a memory test, or a recitation that you are performing, having something to guide and cue you seems eminently sensible.

Everyone has insecurities about their performances, whatever arena they might be in. I once worked with a film actor who most of the UK population of the time would have recognized. He would tell us that even at this point in his long career he would arrive at the film studio expecting someone to tell him there had been some terrible mistake and that he was not the actor they required.

Perhaps it's quite healthy that we don't get too big for our boots and think we are indispensable. But we mustn't forget that no one else can do the speech the way the we can do it, or tell the story with our particular qualities. Nor can anyone else build a relationship like we can. If you have been chosen to speak in a situation it's because you have something unique to offer.

When we do find that confident speaking moment something wonderful happens which we can't wait to repeat. The feeling of being able to express yourself freely and clearly is incredibly empowering, and the more you do it, the more you'll achieve it. So what are you waiting for? It's time to get out there and become the speaker you've always wanted to be.

Appendix:
Speaker's Toolkit

Everyone has their own concerns and preoccupations when it comes to confident speaking. You might want your voice to sound confident when inside you feel a bit wobbly. You might have been told that you sound just fine but don't look particularly relaxed when you speak in a meeting. You might admit that sometimes when you speak the consonants get a bit mumbled, or that when you're nervous all the vowels are shortened and your voice sounds jumpy and ill-at-ease. Whatever your problem, have a look through this toolkit of short and simple exercise ideas to find the solution. Treat it like a menu – what do you have a taste for today? You can do some of the exercises almost anywhere without drawing attention to yourself. For others you might like to find a private corner for a minute or two. If you were a fly on the wall you'd probably catch your favourite actor or singer doing exactly the same exercises when they prepare for their big moment.

1. I want to relax my throat

A relaxed throat will make it easier for you to find power and clarity in your voice. Put the tip of your tongue on the back of your upper teeth – imagine you were about to say the word 'light' or 'love'. Keep your tongue tip in position as you breathe in and out for twenty seconds. It should help you relax. It might even make you want to yawn, which is a great way to open up the throat spaces. Find someone to speak to immediately once you've finished your twenty seconds. Your voice should feel much more relaxed.

2. I want some clear consonants

For this exercise you need to say phrases where each word begins with the same consonant. To make that beginning consonant, two parts of your mouth need to touch. You can speak the words out loud, or mouth them silently:

Ladies loudly laughing love lingering
(Your tongue tip touches the back of your upper teeth.)

Fifty feathers fit for frozen forests
(Your upper teeth touch your lower lip.)

Various virtuous volunteers vanquish vermin
(Your upper teeth touch your lower lip.)

Thirty thick theatrical thieves thumped thirteen thugs
(Your upper teeth touch the upper side of the tongue.)

Wise wives whistle watching white wolves
(Your lips meet.)

The consonants at the beginning of each word in the next six phrases are all plosive: the two parts of your mouth start together then move apart:

Peter painted Paul's purple pullover pink
(Your lips meet.)

Ben built bold black bathrooms
(Your lips meet.)

Kevin caught Cathy's cold canoeing
(The back of your tongue touches the roof of your mouth.)

Gary gave Graham gold glasses
(The back of your tongue touches the roof of your mouth.)

Tiny Tony taught two terriers
(Your tongue tip touches the back of your upper teeth.)

David decided Donald deserved donuts
(Your tongue tip touches the back of your upper teeth.)

These next phrases cover the three nasal consonants. In the first two focus on the long, nasal sound at the beginning of each word:

My mother's mobile murmurs miraculously
(Your lips meet.)

Nine noblemen nibble nuts noisily
(Your tongue tip touches the back of your upper teeth.)

In this third phrase, the 'ng' sound comes at the end of each word:

Sing swing bring long lingering spring
(The back of your tongue touches the roof of your mouth.)

3. I'd like my voice to be friendlier

This exercise can help you find the warmest and most generous tone for your voice. Singers often use the idea of 'inner smiles' and 'outer smiles'. An 'outer smile' would mean that you'd be standing there with a grin on your face, which might not be appropriate to your situation. But an 'inner smile' will help to bring out the warmest colours in your voice. Focus on something or someone that makes you smile inside – a place where you feel safe and cosy, the nicest thing anyone ever said to you. Keep smiling inside as you give a greeting or tell your colleagues how excited you are to be giving your presentation.

4. I need to relax and stand tall

Do you feel a little anxious or apprehensive about a forthcoming event? Does your body feel tight, almost as if you're shrinking in to yourself? Do you quite fancy hiding away or diving for cover? We need to get you grounded and breathing and stretched out so you will look good and confident speaking in front of your audience.

Stand with your back against a wall, your feet about hips' width apart. At all times keep your feet flat on the floor. Look down as you begin to bend your knees: make sure that they are positioned over your toes, and not swaying out to the sides. Gently push your heels down into the floor as you straighten your legs. Bend the knees again and come back up, gently pushing your heels into the floor. Repeat the bending and straightening three more times.

Stand tall against the wall for ten seconds and imagine that your shoulders are very heavy – let them drop a few centimetres. With your back still against the wall imagine that you are growing upwards a couple of centimetres. Stand tall for five more seconds and then step away from the wall. Stand tall and prepare to enter your meeting.

5. I need to find some energy

Been sitting at a computer for the last few hours? Feeling a little lacking in the energy you need to be fully present in your meeting? Find some stairs, and gently jog up and down for the next 30 seconds. You don't need to go fast, but you do need to be aware of your foot touching the step. As you alternate between your right foot and left foot, gently pant with light and quite short out-breaths. If you feel comfortable making some sound you could softly say 'fff … fff … fff … fff' as you jog. By doing this you're waking up your body, waking up your breathing muscles and allowing your body to ground itself, which means you will sound and look more confident in your event. If there's no convenient staircase or your footwear isn't suitable for running up and down you can do some light jogging on the spot.

Now we're going to look at some exercises you can do while driving in the car. I'll presume that you are alone in the car, but if you do have a travel companion you could help each other by giving some practical feedback.

6. I want to warm my voice up

Remember that vocal muscles appreciate exercise just like the other muscles of the body. Turn on the radio or play some music and sing along and you will warm up your voice. Many songs have a wider vocal range than we usually use, so you'll extend your range, and songs also often have a stronger rhythmic energy than we use in speech. You can use all of these new skills when you speak.

7. I want high notes and low notes

Think about some favourite songs. When the singer goes for a higher note, or drops to a low note, doesn't it relate to the words they are singing and the emotion of the song? We can use higher and lower notes when we speak, to make our message more powerful and more deeply engaging.

Play some music and sing along. When you get to a higher note in the song hang on to it – at this point you might want to turn the music off for a few moments. Sing that higher note again, and then on the same note sing the numbers one to five. Now speak the numbers trying to keep in that 'high gear' by speaking in the higher part of your voice. You could then sing and speak the first five or six words of your presentation, or a 'welcome' and 'hello' and introduction you might use in a meeting. Sing on the one high note and then without pausing for breath speak the same five- or six-word phrase. How does that feel, and sound? Does the higher pitch allow you to sound brighter, livelier, more convincing? Turn the music back on and sing for a while until you find some low notes. Do the same exercise as you did with the high pitches. How does your speaking voice sound now? More heavyweight, more authoritative, more serious?

I hope it is obvious, that we all have our limits as to how high or low our voice will comfortably go: if your voice hurts or aches, stop. Next time don't go quite so high or low.

8. I want rhythmic energy

Rhythm can immediately lift our energy and even make us want to sing or dance. In the same way, we might want our audience to be moved to action by our words, and at the very least, a lack of rhythmic energy in our speech can kill our message stone dead.

Turn on your music, find something with a strong rhythm and begin to hum. Turn off the music, but keep humming your strong rhythm. Introduce some words – it could be a series of numbers, or what you need to say at the beginning of your meeting or presentation. Then sing some phrases keeping the strong rhythmic energy. Stop singing and begin to speak your phrases, but keeping the rhythm strong. Speak the phrases again, this time just focussing on the message: can you still hear the echo, the memory of the rhythm, in the background? Does it give a different energy to your message? Might that stronger rhythm make your message stronger or more specific? Matching the right rhythm to the right message is obviously crucial. Try using the same phrases of words with the rhythm of a different piece of music, and see how it affects the message.

9. I want better articulation

Listen to the radio and repeat a phrase that you hear, first out loud and then silently shaping the sounds of the words. It's usually easier to be aware of how well we are articulating when we mouth the words in silence. When we speak out loud the sound of our voice tends to take most of our attention. Simply be aware of the movements made by various parts of your tongue, your lips, and your teeth: if these moves are sluggish you probably won't sound either clear or very interesting.

10. I want to stress the right word

When we stress a word we're telling the audience that this is the most important part of a phrase or sentence. Speak a phrase of no more than seven words that you've heard on the radio and decide to stress just one of those words. Try stressing the first word of the phrase; does that sound good? Is that what you want to say? Repeat the exercise and each time choose a different word to stress. What do you want your audience to understand? The more you practise this exercise the better you will get at sounding as if you've really thought about what you want to communicate.

11. I want speed control

Repeat a couple of sentences you've heard on the radio, dividing them into short four or five word sections. Speak them out loud, pausing at the end of each little section. Repeat the phrases silently, the first section very slow, then the second section fast. Continue with another slow section followed by a fast section. Continue to the end of the final phrase – slow, fast, slow, fast. Speak the phrases out loud again, this time trying to match the speed to the message: you want the fact that you're speaking quickly or slowly to relate to what you want to communicate. Do you feel that you are in control of your pace? Are the words either running away with you or so slow that you lose energy? Are you using the changes in speed to communicate dynamically?

12. I want volume control

Find another phrase from the radio, or use some words you need to speak at work or as part of an event. You don't want to either blast everyone's ears off or be so soft people strain to hear, and you want to vary the volume at which you speak throughout. Sing a short phrase of words gently on one note. Then give yourself time to breathe so you can sing the same phrase twice as loud.

Repeat the exercise – first version soft, second version loud. Pick up another phrase and string them together. The first phrase will be soft, and the new phrase will be loud. Don't sing so loud that you hurt your throat. Now speak the phrases, the first one soft, the second one loud. Does that sound good? Would you like to try the first phrase loud and the second phrase soft, instead? Sing them, then speak them. Does that sound better? Are you hearing some good drama in your delivery through varying the dynamics?

There are lots of variations on this exercise. For example, you could take six very short phrases, and sing them, each one getting progressively louder. How does that sound? Can you keep starting soft and getting louder when you speak the same phrases? Does it help you to feel you are confidently in charge of the words?

Here are some super quick exercises to do when you need a speedy confident speaking boost.

13. I want to speak my name clearly and confidently when I get into my meeting

Silently shape the sounds of the phrase, 'Hello, my name is …' three times, then, if circumstances allow, speak the phrase out loud.

14. I want to sound confident and strong in my meeting even if my energy feels low

Take the phrase, 'I feel on top of the world.' Silently shape the words three times as you look up towards the ceiling. Imagine that the energy of the words is shooting straight through the ceiling, into the room above or out into the open air. Now speak the phrase out loud.

15. I want to ground myself in a meeting when I feel my thoughts are wandering

Take this phrase and say it in your head three times: 'Sixty-seven symmetrical sausages sizzle sensationally.' You'll need to think it through slowly and silently shape each word with care. Now take a breath and focus back on your meeting.

16. I want to lift my spirits so that my voice sounds brighter and more joyful

Take this phrase and shape the words three times silently: 'I feel like laughing out loud.' Imagine you are singing rather than speaking. Now take a breath and speak the phrase out loud.

17. I want to relax my tight shoulders

Put your hands behind your back and interlace your fingers, then lift your hands as high as you comfortably can. Breathe in and imagine you're trying to hit the wall in front of you with your sharp out-breath, and at the same time let the hands part and drop down by your sides.

18. I want to energize my voice after sitting at a computer for hours

Find someone to talk to across as large a space as possible: project a greeting or a question to them, continue a conversation with them for 30 seconds.

19. I want to stretch out my back so that I feel stronger and more commanding

Sit with interlaced fingers on the back of your head, and then alternate gently lifting each elbow. Continue for ten seconds. Unlock your hands, let them come back down by your sides and feel how wide your back is now as you breathe in.

20. I want to warm up my articulation on the bus or train

Put your earphones in, listen to a song and silently shape the words you hear. Then turn the music off and silently shape the content of your speech or the message you need to deliver at the meeting.

21. I want to be heard in a noisy atmosphere like a bar

Find a private corner at home, just for a couple of minutes. Say the 'nyuh' sound you'd find in the middle of the word 'onion'. Now sing those sounds on a medium to high pitch. Put a thumb and the finger next to it either side of your nose and gently massage your nose as you sing. And yes, anyone watching or listening to you might think you've finally lost it! But if you spend some regular time with this one you'll find some nasal resonance that will help your voice ride over all the other noises. It could be useful in noisy meetings too.

22. I want to impress someone with my confidence

Look them in the eye as you talk to them. Practise on simple interactions like 'Hello' and 'How was your holiday?'

Index

A

accent
  being judged on your
    19–22
  good 22
alcohol, dehydrating effect
    of 32
anxiety 169, 172
articulation 5, 10, 13–21,
    135, 162, 194, 198
  exercises 14–18
  muscles 10, 13, 17
audience
  engaging the 80–1
  understanding 44
  perception of you and
    your message 139–42
audience script 74–5
  advantage of 74
audio diary, recording 59
audio material 38
audio recording, *see also*
    voice recorder, 92, 182

B

birthday parties and
    speeches 120–1
breathing 7–12
  and lying flat 12, 28
and stress-levels 8, 166
as a kind of affirmation
    166
basic 179
deep breathing 4, 9, 76–7,
    179–80, 191
exercises 1, 8–12
hyperventilation 172
muscles 4, 9, 77, 179, 191
patterns 171–2
tendency to stop when
    distracted 8
to relax tension 13

C

chest resonance, *see also*
    gravitas, 27
chest, upper, relaxing 10–11
clarity 14–21, 33, 63, 187
coffee, dehydrating effect
    of 32
confidence 4, 9–10, 13, 18,
    45, 60, 65, 76–7, 83,
    111, 127, 131, 198
consonants
  beginning 188
  clear 20
  nasal 189
control, losing, fear of 14

conversations 165–78
    formal 175–6
criticism, constructive 71
cue cards 55, 68, 92, 95
CV
    putting together a 156–8
    verbal overview of 157–8

D
deep breathing 4, 9, 76–7,
    179–80, 191
diction 13–14, 20–1, 33
    good 20
'Do Not Block Your Partner'
    game 173–4

E
energized and relaxed,
    balance between 76
'Energy Builder' exercises
    68–9
energy
    channel, imagining a 178
    performance 177
    rhythmic 5, 23, 33, 192–3
    vocal 59, 178
eulogy, doing a 120
eye contact, importance of
    167–9

F
family-oriented events 120
feelings, voicing your 59

feet, focus on your 77
floor, lying on the
focusing on your subject 62
formal conversations 175–6
friends, practising
    presentations with 71–2
Full Script 75
funerals 120, 90

G
getting your message across
    81
gravitas 27–9
groom's speech 98–112

H
hands
    self-consciousness about
    66
    what to do with your 66–7
humming
    as a vocal warm-up 78
    exercises 31–2, 132, 78,
    178, 193
humour, sense of
hyperventilation 172

I
images, using, *see*
    PowerPoint
interviews, job 151–63
    importance of answering
    all questions 159–60

preparing for 151–9
selling yourself at 161

J
job interviews, *see*
  interviews, job

K
key words or phrases 68

L
language
 spoken 4
 written 4, 81
layout 53–6
leaving speech
 generating material
  141–3
 speech, planning 139–41
linking words, removing 81

M
material, generating 141–3
meditation 153
meetings 165–78
 overall objective in
  attending 165–6
memorial services 120
microphone(s) 73–4
 clip-on, benefits of 73
 hand-held 73
 limitations of 73–4
mind, 'chattering' 152

mirror, watching yourself in
  15–16, 21, 63
monologues 154–5, 160, 168
'Motorway' technique 53–5,
  100
mumbling and muttering 13,
  105
muscles
 articulation 10, 13, 17
 stomach 77
music
 and vocal colour 24, 171
 background 176
 singing along with 31,
  192–3
musical pitch 27

N
nervousness 166, 172

P
pace 17, 19, 128, 195
passion 1, 13, 43–4, 59–60,
  63, 143–4
performance space 73, 78–9
 entering 78–9
Performer Script 75
pictures or diagrams, using
  49
pitch, musical 27
poetry
 comprehension exercise
  124–7

poetry (continued)
  reading 123–4
  rhythm exercise 131–2
PowerPoint 2, 44, 46, 184
  problems 44
  using 44–7
preparation(s) 73–82
  exercises 76–8
  final 57
  focusing on the subject
    of 62
  materials 65, 73
  playing different 'roles'
    37
  practising 71
  preparing and planning
    33–5
  scripting 35, 49–57
  structuring 51–3
  text 62–7
pronunciation 16, 21
prose, reading exercise
    132–5
public speaking 2, 85, 91,
    150
punctuation 94, 127–8

Q
Q&A sessions 69–71

R
radio interview 175
reading, doing a 123–36

recording 3–4, 37–9, 49, 59–
    62, 91–2, 105, 154–8,
    161, 182
rehearsal 2, 35, 49, 56, 65,
    67, 71, 92, 111, 120
  definition of 60
relaxation 4, 27
relaxation exercises for
    gravitas 27–9
resonance 27, 29, 198
rhythm 23–5, 123, 131–2,
    170
  and energy of words 24
  exercise 25
  lifeblood of our message
    23–5
  natural 23

S
'Sandwich' exercise 70–1
scene, setting the 75
screen, using, see also
    PowerPoint 44–6, 66,
    73, 184–5
script, word-for-word 111
scripts, types of 75
self-consciousness while
    speaking 66
self-criticism 4
selling yourself 161–2
shoulders 66–7, 76, 191, 197
  relaxing tension in 66–7
situations, social 79

small talk 173–4
smiles, inner and outer 190
social situations 79
soliloquy 154
Speaker's Toolkit 2, 31–3, 179, 183, 187
speaking
    at different speeds 18
    exercise 61–5
    style, 176, 180
    tips for confident 179–81
speech(es)
    best man' 88, 112–121
    delivering 59–72
    father of the bride's 95–8
    groom's 98–112
    leaving 139–50
    rhythm of 23–4
    wedding 7, 87–121
statistics 74, 176
stomach 8–11, 28–9, 77
    muscles 77
story, your 34, 39, 42–4, 49–50, 62, 65, 70–1, 80–3
    beginning, middle and end of 43
    constructing your 43
    experimenting with ways to tell 50–1
    giving an overview of 42
    telling your 41–4
stress levels 8, 182
'Stressing Game' exercise 25

syllables
    'light' and 'heavy' 23–4
    stressed and unstressed 23

T
talk, drawing the 'shape' of your 50
tea, dehydrating effect of 32
tension 4, 11, 14, 23, 66
    relaxing 66–7
text
    dividing into sections 135–6
    humming the rhythm of 132
thoughts, clarifying your 57
throat
    dry 30
    'hot potato' space in 64
    relaxed 27–8, 63, 187
    restricted 20
    sore 30
    tense 11–13
tone, appropriate 148
TV interview 175

V
Valentine's day 145–9
venue, finding out about 73
visual aids 49
visual material 38

vocal
    delivery, 59–72
    distress 30
    energy 59
    habits 30
    muscles 31, 183, 192
    patterns 172
    range 63–4, 192
    repertoire 59
    sounds, alternative 183
    training 179
voice
    'unhappy' 29–31
    benefits of recording 37
    colours in your 59–61, 63
    controlling 20
    depth of, see also
        gravitas, 27–32
    finding our best 4, 20
    musical notes in 63–5, 192–3
    pitch 64
    putting passion in 59–60
    recorder 3, 33, 37–9,
        42–3, 59, 71, 93, 98–9,
        113, 135, 142–3, 151,
        154–7, 165, 182
    rising and falling notes in 64
    sound of your 148
    tips for improving 31–2
    tone, appropriate 148
    volume control 174, 195
    warm up by humming 78
    whispering 31

voicing your feelings 59
vowel(s) 20–1
    exercises 21
    sounds 14, 20

W
wandering off-topic, see
        'Motorway' technique
warm up your voice 178, 192
wedding speech(es) 7,
        87–121
    and avoiding alcohol 90
    and jokes 89
    balance between tears
        and laughter 90
    best man's speech 88,
        112–121
    bride's parents 114
    bridesmaids 103, 114
    daughter 91–7, 101, 113
    father of the bride's
        speech 95–8
    function of 88–9
    groom's speech 98–112
    ideal length 88
    reception 101, 114
    what to leave out 89
    writing exercise 93–4
'Windmills' exercise 66–7
words
    and tone of voice 148
    choosing the best 41–7
    rhythmic energy of 24

Notes

You can use the following pages to make your own notes on any of the exercises in the book.

Notes

Notes

Notes

Other titles in
the Practical Guides series

Introducing NLP

Introducing Neurolinguistic Programming takes proven psychological techniques and helps you to use them in the real world. It's packed with exercises and activities so you can get started straight away.

ISBN: 9781848312562
eISBN: 9781848313255

Introducing NLP for Work

Introducing NLP for Work gives you practical knowledge of essential NLP concepts and techniques to help you achieve better results at work and stand out from the crowd. Written by an expert in business coaching, *NLP for Work* teaches you how to use NLP techniques to succeed, enabling you to deal effectively with problems and to master any situation.

ISBN: 9781848313804
eISBN: 9781848313811

Introducing CBT

Introducing Cognitive Behavioural Therapy gives you straightforward, proven techniques from experts in this life-changing therapy. You can understand your behaviour and how to change negative patterns. You can learn to relax and put your worries into perspective. You can manage negative emotions to help you think differently. You can feel better about yourself and start achieving your goals again.

ISBN: 9781848312548
eISBN: 9781848313231

Introducing Mindfulness

Introducing Mindfulness helps you appreciate your life instead of rushing through it. Full of straightforward advice, case studies and step-by-step instructions, this is the perfect start to a happier, more focused and stress-free you.

ISBN: 9781848312555
eISBN: 9781848313750

Introducing Emotional Intelligence

Emotional intelligence is the innate potential to feel, use, communicate, recognize, remember, describe, identify, learn from, manage, understand and explain emotions. People who have a higher level of emotional intelligence do better at work in all sorts of fields and in relationships from marriage to casual friends. *Introducing Emotional Intelligence* explores what emotional intelligence is all about and how you can cultivate a higher EQ for yourself.

ISBN: 9781848314221
eISBN: 9781848314382

Introducing Child Psychology

Introducing Child Psychology takes insights from experts in children's development and explains how they can benefit your family. It's full of case studies and activities to help you guide your child through life's challenges.

ISBN: 9781848312586
eISBN: 9781848313293

Introducing Management

Introducing Management uses expert insights, real-life
case studies and proven techniques to improve your
management skills. It's full of practical exercises to help
you get the best out of others, motivate your team and
manage poor performers.

ISBN: 9781848314016
eISBN: 9781848314252

Introducing Psychology of Success

Introducing Psychology of Success helps you identify what
success means to you, and build day-to-day strategies to
help you reach your goals. This Practical Guide teaches
you to overcome obstacles to succeed, change your life
for the better and learn to appreciate the bigger picture.

ISBN: 9781848312593
eISBN: 9781848313316

Introducing Self-Esteem

Introducing Self-Esteem brings you easy-to-follow
techniques for improving your self-image. It's packed with
practices from CBT and related disciplines so you can
achieve a realistic and positive view of yourself and live a
happier and more successful life.

ISBN: 9781848313651
eISBN: 9781848313668

Introducing Psychology of Relationships

Understanding psychological techniques can help you make your relationships happier and more fulfilling. *Introducing Psychology of Relationships* will help you achieve new and healthier ways of relating by explaining some of the major underlying psychological 'drivers' that permeate relationships, and to identify and work on these unconscious motivating factors to eliminate 'knee-jerk' reactions.

ISBN: 9781848313590
eISBN: 9781848313606

Introducing Positive Psychology

Positive psychologists seek to find and nurture genius and talent, and to make normal life more fulfilling. This Practical Guide explores how we can all have a 'life of enjoyment', in which we savour the positive emotions that are part of healthy living; a 'life of engagement' where we feel confident we can tackle the tasks we face; and a 'life of affiliation', being part of something larger than ourselves.

ISBN: 9781848312777
eISBN: 9781848313736

Introducing Ethics for Everyday Life

Ethical philosophy has a long and distinguished history, but how can you apply it to your life? *Introducing Ethics for Everyday Life* provides advice on whether human beings really are selfish and greedy, why you might want to be a good person, and how to pick an ethical philosophy that works for you. Full of straightforward advice, case studies and step-by-step instructions, this is the perfect concise introduction to using ethics to help you make decisions.

ISBN: 9781848313415
eISBN: 9781848313712

Introducing Happiness

By looking at the history of thought, this guide will help you do things which support your well-being, free yourself from the various disturbances of life, overcome irrational expectations that cause us distress, and understand the causes of suffering.

ISBN: 9781848313620
eISBN: 9781848313637

Introducing Philosophy for Everyday Life

How can we apply philosophy to our everyday lives? Can philosophy affect the way we live? This book will show how philosophy can help to improve your thinking about everyday life. And how, by improving the quality of your thinking, you can improve the quality of your life. Full of practical examples and straightforward advice, and written by an expert in the field, this guide can help you become calmer and happier, and make better decisions.

ISBN: 9781848313569
eISBN: 9781848313576

Sport Psychology

Introducing Sport Psychology will help you become fitter and stronger, achieve your goals and enjoy exercise, with proven, expert techniques. It's full of practical tips to help you train your mind and improve your health. You can improve your performance whatever your sport or level of fitness, relieve stress and reduce anxiety about life's challenges, recover from injury faster and more effectively, and make exercise a habit to feel better all round.

ISBN: 9781848312579
eISBN: 9781848313279

Introducing Body Language

Introducing Body Language explains how to read other people and how to be more aware of what you are saying with your own body language. This easy-to-read guide teaches you how to understand non-verbal messages, dealing separately with different parts of the body, such as facial expressions, posture and hand movements.

ISBN: 9781848314214
eISBN: 9781848314375

Introducing Assertiveness

Introducing Assertiveness introduces you to key theories and practical techniques to make you more assertive. By helping you to overcome passive behaviour it will enable you to express yourself more clearly in your work and personal life.

ISBN: 9781848315051
eISBN: 9781848315228

Getting the Job You Want

Introducing Getting the Job You Want supports you through all the stages of finding your perfect job – from organization and preparation to the different ways to implement a job search campaign. In a challenging job market you need to create a resumé that will sell you, and to be well prepared for interview. Both new graduates and those returning to the job search will learn simple yet effective techniques from award-winning career psychologist, Denise Taylor.

ISBN: 9781848315068
eISBN: 9781848315242

CBT for Work

Introducing CBT for Work focuses on how you can incorporate CBT's insights to improve your time in the workplace, such as tackling lack of self-motivation or feelings of inadequacy, and replacing them with new ways of thinking that will make you both happier and more effective in your work. Whether you're suffering from a particular complaint or simply feel that CBT's measured and results-driven approach can be of benefit to you, this is the perfect concise guidebook.

ISBN: 9781848314191
eISBN: 9781848314351

Leadership

Introducing Leadership draws on the ideas and strategies of successful leaders from business and wider society to give you tried-and-tested solutions to the conundrums of modern business leadership. You'll discover their ideas and strategies which can be applied to the opportunities and challenges that you face. So whether you're starting from scratch as a new leader, needing to raise your game, or aiming to do what great leaders do and aim even higher, this practical yet inspirational guide will help you to perform at your very best.

ISBN: 9781848315112
eISBN: 9781848315280

Family Psychology

Based on practical, clinically proven, and tried-and-tested approaches, *Introducing Family Psychology* teaches you how to successfully raise a family in today's society. It provides workable solutions based on experiences that cross cultural boundaries. Practical tips alongside real-life case studies offer tried-and-tested solutions to the problems you and your child might face along the way.

ISBN: 9781848315181
eISBN: 9781848315365

Entrepreneurship

Introducing Entrepreneurship offers expert insights, case studies and advice to begin your entrepreneurial journey. It reveals the stories of the world's greatest entrepreneurs, distilling the key points into down-to-earth, realistic advice and practical techniques to help you turn any business opportunity into a successful venture.

ISBN: 9781848316256
eISBN: 9781848316270

Business Creativity

Introducing Business Creativity provides innovative techniques and proven theories to help you improve your creative thinking and get more out of yourself and your business. Whether you are trying to develop entirely new initiatives or redesign the way you operate, this book will help you break out of your old patterns of thought, think outside the box and generate pioneering ideas that you can put into action.

ISBN: 9781848314009
eISBN: 9781848314245

Counselling

Introducing Counselling provides you with expert insights, real-life case studies and practical skills to teach you to talk, listen, support and understand better.

ISBN: 9781848316263
eISBN: 9781848316287

Overcoming Phobias

Introducing Overcoming Phobias helps you understand your fears and free yourself from anxiety. With expert advice, case studies and practical techniques, this is the perfect guide to building a new, phobia-free life.

ISBN: 9781848316508
eISBN: 9781848316904

Emotional Freedom Techniques

Introducing Emotional Freedom Techniques draws on both ancient Chinese wisdom and modern psychology to improve your emotional and physical wellbeing. With expert advice, case studies and techniques, here is a new way to change your life for good.

ISBN: 9781848316621
eISBN: 9781848316966

Introducing the Practical Guides:
Free Ebook Sampler

Read extracts from a selection of Practical Guides with this FREE ebook sampler. Available to download everywhere ebooks are sold or via introducingbooks.com/freesample

eISBN: 9781848314610